David Bryant

Our FORBIDDEN Moon

IS SPACEFLIGHT DENIED TO MANKIND?

OUR FORBIDDEN MOON

Second Edition. Revised and Updated

Copyright © 2020 David Bryant. All rights reserved.

First paperback edition printed 2020 in the United Kingdom.

A catalogue record for this book is available from the British Library.

ISBN 978-1-9997417-3-0

No part of this book shall be reproduced or transmitted in any form or by any means, electronic or mechanical, including photocopying, recording, or by any information retrieval system without written permission of the publisher.

Published by

Heathland Books

For more copies of this book, please email: info@spacerocksuk.com

Telephone: 01603 715933

Designed and typeset by Bob Tibbitts ~ (iSET)

Printed in Great Britain

Although every precaution has been taken in the preparation of this book, the publisher and author assume no responsibility for errors or omissions. Neither is any liability assumed for damages resulting from the use of this information contained within.

Contents

ACKNOWLEDGEMENTS 5

INTRODUCTION 7

FOREWORD BY NICK POPE 11

Chapter 1:
WHAT'S GOING ON HERE? 15

Chapter 2:
SMOKE AND MIRRORS 25

Chapter 3:
THE HIDDEN AGENDA 37

Chapter 4:
THE 'C' WORD! 77

OUR FORBIDDEN MOON

Chapter 5:
OUR FORBIDDEN MOON 81

Appendix 1:
TOO GOOD TO BE TRUE? APOLLO 13 97

Appendix 2:
THE STRANGE CASE OF THE MOONROCKS 103

Appendix 3:
THE DEVIL IS IN THE DETAIL: DUMMIES, BUGGIES AND CGI 107

Appendix 4:
BEGINNINGS 115

Appendix 5:
RENDLESHAM FOREST 123

Appendix 6:
HOW COULD ANYTHING THIS BIG BE KEPT SECRET? 129

GLOSSARY 135

ACKNOWLEDGEMENTS

THIS isn't the Oscars, so let's keep it brief!

There are a few people whose encouragement and help have been central in persuading me to get on and write this book instead of just talking about it:

Paul Williams is a total space nut! He doesn't share any of my misgivings about the Apollo Program, but has nonetheless been a terrific mate and great sounding board; it was he who opened the door to my astronaut encounters.

Jason Hughes started off as a customer and, with his lovely partner Jane and two delightful kids, soon became among my closest of friends. It was he who encouraged me to return to Rendlesham Forest for the 2010 conference, reigniting an interest that goes back to 1983.

David Orbell has researched extensively about the Apollo Program and its inconsistencies. We have sat together discussing his findings in restaurants, bars and coffee shops: he still hasn't picked up the bill! Just a great guy with much to add to the debate: read some of his ideas on *Aulis.com*

OUR FORBIDDEN MOON

And finally:

Linda Bryant, my long-suffering wife (yes, I know every writer uses that phrase, but if you knew me, you'd know it is definitely merited in this case!) I wouldn't have achieved a quarter of the things I have in life without Linda's encouragement, support and occasional raised eyebrow! On many occasions she has trudged around Rendlesham Forest with me on pitch-black nights, listened to me delivering the same lectures a dozen times each and, twenty five years ago, taught me how to use a computer! All the way through this project she has advised me what to include and what to leave out; nevertheless, if the final result is any good, I get the credit!

Linda and David Bryant

INTRODUCTION

ALTHOUGH these days heavily-lined with age and care-worn from a somewhat reckless and hedonistic lifestyle, the face of the man sitting the other side of the desk was familiar to just about everyone on the planet. He watched me checking the operation of the digital recorder positioned between us.

"You know, if it hadn't been for Roswell, you'd've had to have learned shorthand like the reporters in the old days!" He leaned forward, fingers bunched together, thumbs circling each other.

"You good to go?" I nodded

"Well OK then: let's start..."

Checking my notes, I collected my thoughts and spoke:

"Why now? Why after all these years have you decided to come clean about what really happened on the Moon? About what's still happening in space?"

The astronaut considered his response carefully.

"You know I'm dying? I have leukemia. And I'm the wrong side of eighty. We've lost so many of the Apollo guys – Pete, Jim, Al, Neil.... and some of the others can hardly recall their names these days. It's time to put the record straight before there's no-one left who can remember anything."

"Aren't you concerned about your personal safety? What you've told me already is pretty explosive stuff!"

"Well hell: what can they do to me now? And anyhow, by the time you find a publisher – if you can find one – I could be in a plot at Arlington!"

Fair point, I reflected...

"So: tell me all about NASA and the hidden UFO agenda!"

That is the 'on the record' conversation that should form the basis of this account. Sadly, it hasn't taken place, and seems unlikely to do so in the future: the Mercury Astronauts are long gone and, at the time of writing only a fraction of the Gemini crew members are still alive. Just four of the Apollo Moonwalkers and two of their Command Module pilots remain of the eighteen who, according to the history books, flew to the Moon and back between 1969 and 1972. Of these, the youngest, General Charlie Duke was born in 1935, while several of the others are in very poor health.

Since 1957, when, aged six, I had my first encounter with an unidentified flying object, the idea that we might occasionally be visited by craft – or even entities – from other worlds far across the cosmos has fascinated me. Four years later, mankind began to take its first hesitant steps into space, and even at the age of ten I was convinced I wanted to be part of this! Astronomy and astronautics became passions that have lasted my whole life, led me into a brief career as a naval pilot, and a longer one as a lecturer and teacher on space-related topics. Eventually, I became the UK's only full-time dealer in meteorites and space-flown memorabilia....

Through these academic and commercial interests, I have been lucky enough to spend time with a good number of Astronauts and Cosmonauts and have listened attentively to what they have said or hinted at in both public and private conversations. From the very first time I spoke with an Apollo astronaut (Capt James Lovell) I felt certain I was being offered a carefully-sanitized version of events: nothing since has changed that opinion. Given the esteem in which I hold these heroes of the space age, as I reviewed my notes it was painful to identify so many glaring discrepancies in their memories of the various missions they'd flown. Sometimes these were contradictions between their account and those of their fellow-astronauts. Sometimes they contradicted themselves. Sometimes, as a science graduate, I was aware that their stories just didn't make scientific sense. Often it seemed - sometimes unsuccessfully - that they were attempting to recall a script they'd been given to deflect 'difficult' questions. What follows are some critical examples.

OUR FORBIDDEN MOON

FOREWORD

By NICK POPE

WHEN considering the UFO phenomenon, much is made of the opinions of police officers, pilots, military personnel and government officials. Such people are generally regarded as being excellent witnesses if they've had a sighting themselves, as well as being thought of as people who, by virtue of their positions, might have access to a degree of inside knowledge about the phenomenon more generally. Following this logic, there is one category of individuals whose opinions and experiences might reasonably be regarded as even more important: the astronauts and cosmonauts. After all, if Earth is being visited by intelligent extraterrestrials, the most likely place from which to see them, and in which to encounter them, would be space. Additionally, if some governments are guarding a great and terrible secret truth about UFOs, the astronauts may well be in on this secret too, because if there are extraterrestrials out there, it's the astronauts who would be at the sharp end.

Following on from this, a number of important questions arise: Have any astronauts seen UFOs? Were they given information on the subject from NASA or elsewhere? Were we warned off the moon - and did we even go there in the first place? The internet, of course, is full of rumours about such questions, but it's extremely difficult to sort out fact from fiction. The problem is access. Most people have never met any of the astronauts, and if they have, it's likely to have been a fleeting encounter at a book signing event, with limited chances for anything other than a brief sound bite.

The book you now have in your hands is different. David Bryant is a formal naval pilot, and given that many of the astronauts began their careers as military pilots, David has been able to talk to them as an equal. This, coupled with his meteorite and space memorabilia businesses, has given him unprecedented access to the elite astronaut and cosmonaut community. Think of it in terms of being a small and very exclusive club, to which David has a guest membership. In all, he's met over 30 astronauts, including seven of the twelve moonwalkers. This unique access and shared military background means that these people opened up to David in a way that they wouldn't to the media or the public.

The result of all this is the meticulously-researched, fascinating and highly controversial book that you are about to read. And if any of it sounds far-fetched, consider how many mainstream media stories you've seen recently, hinting that it's only a matter of time before we find alien life. Maybe we've already found it. Or maybe it found us.

Nick Pope worked for the Ministry of Defence for 21 years, and from 1991 to 1994 he ran the MoD's UFO project. His final post was as an acting Deputy Director in the Directorate of Defence Security.

OUR FORBIDDEN MOON

The author chats with Mercury, Gemini and Apollo astronauts

. . . and with Shuttle astronauts, controllers and cosmonauts

OUR FORBIDDEN MOON

CHAPTER 1:

When you have eliminated the possible, whatever remains . . .

WHAT'S GOING ON HERE?

LIVING as I do in rural Norfolk, I tend to take for granted the number and brightness of the stars I can see on a typical cloudless night. Even with a bright Moon, I can always see the Milky Way and stars down to fifth magnitude. So dark are the skies here that, on a typical night, I can stand in my driveway **even with the external security and house lights illuminated** and still observe the Milky Way, dim stars, satellites and meteors. And yet Gen. Duke, the Apollo 16 Moonwalker, has frequently claimed in my hearing and in his lectures around the world that the stars are neither visible from cislunar space (between leaving Earth orbit and reaching the Moon) nor from the surface of the Moon itself. This is curious for a number of reasons:

The Institute of Navigation says on its website:

"...where ground tracking was not practical, an on-board inertial navigation system was used. Astronauts periodically used a sextant to sight on stars and the horizons of the Earth and Moon to align the inertial system, and to verify the accuracy of the Earth-based tracking data."

This is, of course, totally at odds with Gen Duke's comments. Again, the

OUR FORBIDDEN MOON

best-known Moonwalker of them all, Neil Armstrong, said in an interview with Patrick Moore on the BBC's *The Sky at Night* in 1970:

"The sky is a deep black when viewed from the Moon, as it is when viewed from cislunar space. The Earth is the only visible object other than the Sun that can be seen."

And yet Apollo 14 Moonwalker Dr Edgar Mitchell has confirmed to me that, in cislunar space

"... the stars are ten times brighter than when viewed from the Earth".

Famously, critical trajectory adjustment rocket firings on the Apollo 13 mission had to rely on sightings of the limb of the Sun: as the NASA website explains:

'Ordinarily the alignment procedure uses an onboard sextant device, called the Alignment Optical Telescope, to find a suitable navigation star, then, with the help of the onboard computer, verify the guidance platform's alignment. However, due to the explosion (of an oxygen tank aboard the Service Module), *a swarm of debris ... made it impossible to sight real stars.'*

There is no credible reason why stars should *not* be seen from the Moon's surface: there is no atmosphere to speak of to scatter Sun – or Earthlight and the lunar regolith, although essentially pale grey and apparently fairly reflective, would not be a factor were an astronaut standing with his back to the Sun or Earth, or in a shadow (as was frequently the case). This is even more true in cislunar space or Earth orbit. Indeed, Shuttle Astronaut Kathy Thornton (veteran of 40 days in Earth orbit) confirmed to me that the stars were

"... much brighter than if viewed from the Earth" adding that she had never needed to use a telescope or binoculars to aid her view of the stars from the Shuttle windows.

OUR FORBIDDEN MOON

There is *one* credible reason why many of the Moonwalkers should perpetuate this unsupportable myth and it seems to have much to do with their photographic efforts on the Moon's surface.

The stills cameras used on lunar surface EVAs were variations on the basic theme of the Hasselblad 500EL. This could be attached to a 'shoe' on the Moonwalker's suit, allowing only the clumsiest attempts at framing and composition of a shot. Exposure guides were printed on top of the film magazines: the shutter speed was set to 1/250, with recommended f-stops of $f/5.6$ for objects in shadow and $f/11$ for those in the Sun. The astronauts knew the exposure bracketing technique that many wildlife and sport photographers use, adjusting the exposures one stop up or down from the initial setting, to guarantee – hopefully – at least one good photograph in a group of three.

Some of you may already be wondering how these adjustments could have been made while wearing multi-layered and virtually inflexible EVA gloves, or you may be reflecting on the astonishing quality of much of the lunar surface photography, given these constraints. However, one thing is certain: with white spacesuits, reflective regolith and bright sunlight, the camera settings must have been such that the desired objects were not over-exposed. This being the case, it would certainly be true that exposure times would be too short and apertures too small to image even bright stars. But that's not the same as saying you couldn't see stars with the human eye. What's more, astronauts are seen in many photographs with their gold-plated helmet visors retracted, making it even more likely that they could have hardly avoided noticing the incredibly bright stars in the pitch black lunar sky.

As early as 1969, voices of dissent were already suggesting that there was something not quite *kosher* about the Moon landings: I suggest that NASA anticipated critical questions about the lack of stars in lunar surface images and, perhaps not trusting the astronauts to give a clear explanation of the intricacies of camera setting on the Moon, gave them a stock response to learn:

"You can't see stars on the Moon or in cislunar space"

Possibly, over 50 years later, some have forgotten this, or more likely have recognised the basic implausibility of the explanation. Others have publically reiterated it too often to back down.

There is, naturally, another possibility: the photographs were taken in a studio on Earth!

That is not necessarily to say that the Moon landings did not take place, rather that some or all of the photographs were fabricated for reasons I shall explore further on.

In correspondence with me before his death in 2011, Group Six Apollo astronaut Dr Brian O'Leary was prepared to admit:

"If some of the film was spoiled, it's possible that NASA may have shot some scenes in a studio environment to avoid embarrassment."

More interestingly, if you correlate the amount of photos allegedly taken on the Moon with the time available to do so, the results are quite surprising:

        Apollo 11 – 1 EVA .... 151 minutes

        Apollo 12 – 2 EVAs .... 470 minutes

        Apollo 14 – 2 EVAs .... 565 minutes

        Apollo 15 – 3 EVAs .... 1110 minutes

        Apollo 16 – 3 EVAs .... 1214 minutes

        Apollo 17 – 3 EVAs .... 1324 minutes

OUR FORBIDDEN MOON

EVA time on the Moon totalled 4834 minutes, while 5771 photographs taken were taken. That's **one photograph every 50 seconds!**

No time to sleep, collect rocks, eat, drive the Moon Rover . . .

So why might some of these images have been generated on Earth? Let's explore the possibilities!

Watch the birdie!

The EVA (extra-vehicular activity) spacesuits used by the Apollo Moonwalkers were clumsy, heavy and virtually inflexible: this was particular the case with the gloves worn on the lunar surface. Apollo 17 geologist 'Jack' Harrison Schmitt recalled:

"I had been aware from the experience of previous crews that you could get rough or damaged finger tips and that your fingernails could lift right off the quick as a result of constantly reaching in the suit and getting a little bit of grabbing from the rubber bladder. Knowing that, I wore some nylon liners and also kept my fingernails clipped down as far as possible to delay the process. But, ultimately, all my nails were lifted off the quick and I can remember seeing blood under Gene's fingernails. There was nothing much else you could do about it; it was just a continuous, traumatic soreness which faded into the background."

(I shall return to this astonishing statement later!)

Given the above, there is little doubt that the astronauts would have experienced problems using the bulky Hasselblad 500 cameras: in fact, the most striking thing about the NASA lunar landing archive is *just how good many of the photos are!* They are often perfectly composed and with pin-sharp focus and studio-quality illumination of the subject. (The famous image of Buzz Aldrin taken by Neil Armstrong is a case in point. In many other shots the horizon reflected in an astronaut's visor lines up perfectly with the background horizon: no mean feat given the inability to see the viewfinder with the camera positioned on the photographer's chest!) Compare the hundreds of beautiful still images with the grainy, jerky out of focus video of Armstrong descending to the lunar surface from the Apollo 11 LM. Would the American people have felt their 23 billion dollars (the audited cost of the entire Apollo program) had been well spent had the quality of stills photography been no better? I doubt it... In fact, one of the main reasons given for the cancellation of the Moon landings after Apollo 17 with three further missions ready to go is that the US public had grown bored with the whole idea as early as 1970, when the launch of Apollo 13 was not even picked up by the main TV networks. The need to fabricate images to satisfy the media and general public would certainly explain Dr O'Leary's earlier comment.

Cameras, film and radiation

It has long been central to the arguments of those who dispute the reality of the Moon landings that conventional film cameras could not possibly function on the harsh, radiation-swept lunar surface. As most people will know, X-rays and other high energy electromagnetic radiations will fog conventional emulsions: that's why it's not a great idea to pass film stock, loaded cameras or exposed film through airport security X-ray scanners!

Lacking a protective atmosphere like the Earth's, the Moon receives high levels of ultraviolet, X-ray and infra-red radiation from the Sun, as well as potentially far more damaging cosmic radiation. This constant influx of protons, neutrons and alpha particles is generally thought to have originated in supernovae or active galactic nuclei. It is a major concern to those planning a mission to Mars, simply because months of exposure to it might well prove fatal: it has already been shown that cosmic rays caused a malfunction of the Voyager 2 space craft in 2010.

Another factor is the extreme temperature encountered on the Moon: During the lunar day the temperature on the Moon reaches 250° Fahrenheit (120° Celsius), far in excess of what would be needed to damage photographic films or their colour emulsions. Furthermore, in shadow lunar temperatures drop to -380° Fahrenheit (-230° Celsius). So an astronaut has only to turn 180° away from the Sun to subject his camera to a rapid temperature change of over 400°C! Of course, the H500 cameras were given a reflective surface and the film cassettes had some additional thermal protection, but even so, one would imagine some images (or whole strips of film) might have been affected. But that was not recorded to have been the case!

An indication of the problem these temperature differentials caused the Apollo astronauts comes from Apollo 15 CM Pilot, Col. Al Worden. Despite the shiny, highly reflective surface of all three modules of the Apollo spacecraft, Worden stated in interview:

"We had a little problem with thermal heating on the way out and on the way back from the Moon. If you stay in one attitude and let the sun shine on just one side of the spacecraft, you've got a big problem because the temperature on that surface is going to go up to about 350 degrees and the temperature on the other side, on the shadow side is going to drop to about minus 250. So you've got a 600 degree temperature differential and I don't think anyone trusted it that much. So what we did on the way out, we had the Lunar Module stuck on our nose and we turned perpendicular to the plane of the ecliptic and we just slowly rotated, about once every two minutes just to keep that heating rate constant around the spacecraft.

Of course the terminology for that was 'the barbecue manoeuvre': kind of true! So that's how we took care of the thermal issue on the way out to the Moon. Once we got into Lunar orbit it wasn't so bad, because we're only seeing the sun for half a revolution."

So is it credible that nearly six thousand photographs were successfully

OUR FORBIDDEN MOON

AS14-64-9089, version 1 above, version 2 below. The impossible brightness of Edgar Mitchell's suit and the unconvincing shadows – both suggestive of an artificial light source – have been doctored!

exposed on the Moon with no adverse affects from the solar and cosmic radiation and the intense heat and cold of the Moon?

There are a couple of final points to make about the purported Apollo lunar images. When I first started giving talks about the Apollo landings, I naturally downloaded several hundred 'public domain' images from the NASA website for use in *Powerpoint* presentations. Occasionally I would need to alter the contrast to bring out extra detail or features hidden in shadow. To my surprise, I began to discover anomalous outlines, unexpected structures and lighting inconsistencies: these files were saved on my hard drive for later consideration. A couple of years later I decided to download higher definition copies of the same images, only to find that many of them had been 'improved'.

Why should this have been done? Quite possibly to counter the careful photographic analysis of researchers like Jack White, who uncovered literally hundreds of incongruities in the NASA photographic catalogue.

Back in the late nineties when I bought my first PC and connected it to the internet via a dial-up modem, it would take ages to download an item from the NASA website: most people (including me!) didn't persevere. What's more, image handling software such as Paintshop or Photoshop was incredibly expensive, so NASA had no need to worry about being caught out! I can imagine the consternation at the Cape when PC magazines began to give away light versions of these programs on their cover discs!

OUR FORBIDDEN MOON

CHAPTER 2:

SMOKE AND MIRRORS

MAYBE NASA knew that conventional photography was impossible on the Moon and generated all the images in their archives in a secure location on Earth: certainly many strange anomalies have been discovered by researchers.

Interesting anecdote time! Some years ago, I gave a lecture about the Moon landings to members of an astronomical society in Bedford: the meeting took place in the laboratories of a famous public school. At the end of the talk an elderly lab assistant was helping clear up when he amazed me by saying:

"I met Neil Armstrong once! He and Buzz Aldrin were practising for the Moon landings at Cardington."

(Cardington is a village near Bedford that has two truly enormous aircraft hangers. These were intended for the construction of giant airships (the notorious R101 was built there) but have had a range of uses since, both military and civilian.)

Since there is absolutely no record of any such training taking place in the UK, I was intrigued and pressed the old gentleman for more details.

OUR FORBIDDEN MOON

"I worked there at the time as a technician: the hangars were used for fire testing, constructing blimps and so on. They built a fantastically accurate film full-scale model of the Moon's surface – it had little craters, boulders, a Lunar Module: everything. Armstrong & Aldrin used it to practise putting up equipment, climbing in and out of the module and so on. It was very realistic and totally hush-hush, of course!"

When I later realised the implications of this casually-delivered bombshell, I tried to get in touch with the lab. tech., but he'd retired and moved away...

Is this proof that the Moon landings never occurred?

Has NASA and the American government been lying to us since the start of the Apollo program?

The technician's testimony **on its own** is more suggestive of a desperate

OUR FORBIDDEN MOON

need to produce high-quality images for the media in advance of the Apollo 11 landing, as described above. But there *is* evidence that suggests we may all have been hoodwinked!

I don't propose to go through every piece of anomalous data here: there are literally thousands of online resources and books devoted to the subject, some better-researched than others. But there are a few worth considering within the context of this document.

Silent running: the LM descent motor

As I have indicated above, my time in the Royal Navy was very brief: to be honest, I washed out (as they say) during flying training, following a spell in hospital with a bout of pneumonia. But in between the tedious repetition of 'circuits and bumps' in de Havilland Chipmunks, I also spent precious hours in aircraft familiarity operations. These were wonderful experiences for an aviation and space-crazy twenty year-old: I had the opportunity to carry out 'nav-exes' in Wasp, Sea King and Wessex helicopters. Best of all, though: I got to ride as a passenger in a two-seat Hawker Hunter T8 jet fighter! What most surprised me is how noisy things get during takeoff, even when wearing earplug comms and a 'bone dome'. As an indication of just **how** noisy: a US F-16 fighter at take off generates **145db**. This is several times louder than a thunderclap or an air raid siren and is, of course, produced by an engine just a short distance behind the pilot's head.

What does this have to do with the Moon landings?

Over the years I have had the opportunity to discuss the lunar descent phase of the Apollo missions with several astronauts who, apparently, still vividly recall the details of their ten or so minute ride down to the Moon's surface.

According to Capt. Alan Bean and Gen. Charles Duke the descent is quiet, with some occasional vibration and dull thumps, because, as Gen Duke told me:

OUR FORBIDDEN MOON

"You're in an airless environment: there's no atmosphere to carry the sound of the descent stage engine to the cabin. The loudest noise is from the life support system"

On one amazing occasion, I was seated between Capt. Gene Cernan (commander of the Apollo 17 mission and last man to walk on the Moon) and Apollo 12 astronaut Alan Bean: I questioned both separately about their memories of the Lunar descent phase. Bean more or less echoed Duke's comments, even growing a little exasperated when I pressed him on the point, retorting:

"Who went to the damn Moon? You or me? You're in a vacuum and you can't hear anything outside!"

Ten minutes later, when I put the same question to Cernan, his response was the complete opposite!

"The descent is like sitting in a barrel with guys banging on the outside with hammers. It's real noisy with heavy vibration at times."

Can this apparent contradiction be explained? Not easily: the noise and vibration of the 10,125lb thrust descent stage engine would be communicated to the crew compartment via the various support brackets and struts connecting the engine to the framework of the Lunar Module. It is the case that the engine was throttled down to 65% power much of the time to limit nozzle erosion, but remember: the astronauts are standing on an aluminium honeycomb floor just a couple of centimetres thick. In his book 'A Man On The Moon' Andrew Chaikin wrote:

"In the ascent stage, the walls of the crew cabin were thinned down until they were nothing more than a taut aluminium balloon, in some places only five-thousandths of an inch thick. Once, a workman accidentally dropped a screwdriver inside the cabin and it went through the floor."

This material is all that separated the crew from the descent stage! If anything, Cernan may have **understated** the noise and vibration!

OUR FORBIDDEN MOON

It is true that the astronauts within the LM wore spacesuits and helmets during descent (given that Alan Bean told me that the skin of the spacecraft was the thickness of *"...a sheet of baking foil"*, that's perhaps, not surprising!) but even so, it seems that either some of the Moonwalkers are not telling the truth, or can no longer recall critical moments of the defining events of their lives!

Some years ago I asked Shuttle Astronaut Mark Kelly what launch and ascent to orbit felt like. He replied that it was:

"Like a twenty minute train wreck: the noise and vibration – even through your flight suit and helmet – is intense: you're just about holding on. This only stops after MECO (main engine cut-off) It's the reason some rookies wear diapers for their first mission!'

Dust and craters!

Even before President Kennedy pledged that America would put a man on the Moon before the end of the sixties, science fiction writers had been imagining such an event for decades. In the very year of Kennedy's bold promise, Arthur C Clarke published 'A Fall of Moondust', in which a tourist 'bus' on the Moon sinks deeply into the talcum powder-like lunar regolith. In fact, every artistic rendering of a Moon landing in most of the NASA publications produced during these exciting times shows clouds of fine dust being thrown up by rocket exhaust, leaving behind a deepish crater.

Anticipation of such a surface was the main reason for the wide circular pads at the end of each of the LM's landing legs. It was even considered possible that an LM might dig a crater into which it might tip, preventing the planned return to lunar orbit by the ascent stage! And yet EVA photographs show only a very thin layer of dust, just thick enough to display footprints and tyre tracks made by the Lunar Rovers: even this is absent in many images. Strangely, however, in *every* lunar surface photo there is not a speck of dust on the LM's landing pads, nor the LM itself.

Neil Armstrong himself commented that the surface was:

"...fine and powdery" and continued: *"Okay. The descent engine did not leave a crater of any size. It has about one foot clearance on the ground. We're essentially on a very level place here."*

How could this be? In his taut commentary during the final few metres of Apollo 11's descent to the Moon, Buzz Aldrin makes the taciturn comment:

"Kicking up some dust!"

...and the live video transmitted at the time shows this to be the case. Yet still photos of this landing site and of all five others show little if any evidence of cratering or disturbance under the LM! It is admittedly the case that the descent stage motor was shut off just before touchdown:

Contact light... OK: engine stop!

This sequence was initiated by one of three lunar surface sensing probes: in other words the motor, still running at 3000lb thrust, wasn't shut down until it was less than two metres above the surface of the Moon. Would you fancy standing two metres from a howling rocket exhaust at 3000lb thrust running at close to 5000°C ?

Apollo apologists insist the blast from the engine would not have excavated a crater, displaced dust onto the LM or produced any evidence of melting on the surface under the LM, but this goes against both common sense and the online film evidence of engine tests and rocket launches. The area beneath any large US rocket is protected by a flame trench into which thousands of litres of water are sprayed to cool the launch pad and protect the vehicle from blast. Yet during the landing and lunar ascent phases the Apollo lander had no such protection. Type 'Apollo LM Falcon lift off' into your search engine to watch a video of the A15 ascent stage igniting and leaving the Moon: it is hard to see how the reflected blast of the ascent stage motor didn't damage the flimsy spacecraft.

OUR FORBIDDEN MOON

An image of the Apollo 17 Lunar Rover, following the repair of one of its fenders with cardboard and duct tape. Lots of footprints, but where are the tyre tracks?

The skip re-entry contradiction

In 2014 David Orbell, a delegate at talks given in Birmingham by two Apollo astronauts (Gen. Tom Stafford, Apollo 10 and Col. Al Worden, Apollo 15) asked each a question about the re-entry techniques used by the Command Module during its return to Earth.

OUR FORBIDDEN MOON

As anyone old enough to remember the Moon landings or who has watched the film 'Apollo 13' may recall, the Apollo spacecraft was not re-usable like the five Shuttle Orbiters: it was a single-mission expendable vehicle. Having returned to Earth from the Moon, the Command Module carrying the three astronauts separated from the Service Module before realigning itself for re-entry through the Earth's atmosphere. Following the nine Apollo lunar missions, (including the six successful landings) the Command Modules were travelling at velocities approaching 40,000 k/h as they approached Earth. This compares with the 28,000 k/h of an orbiting spacecraft such as the Shuttle, Gemini or Mercury. The heatshield of the Apollo CM was made of an ablative material designed to convert kinetic energy into heat and dissipate it into space.

According to Chris Kraft, Senior Flight Director during the Apollo Missions, the high velocity of the incoming CMs precluded a 'straight in' approach: instead a re-entry profile known as **skip re-entry** had to be used. This involved the spacecraft dipping in and out of the atmosphere a number of times to dissipate some of the kinetic energy before final re-entry and splash down in the ocean.

Orbell asked Stafford and Worden if the skip entry procedure had caused any problems: both astronauts replied that the missions had ended with a

'...straight in, six and a half degree re-entry.'

Orbell then read out the relevant quote from Kraft's article in 'Popular Mechanics'

"The heat-shield requirements would be too great. So what we did was get them into the atmosphere, skip it out to kill off some of the velocity, and then bring it back in again. That made the total heat pulse on the heat shield of the spacecraft considerably lower."

To the amazement of the audience, both astronauts claimed that the Senior Flight Director was mistaken. Col. Worden added:

OUR FORBIDDEN MOON

"Chris Craft is a bad guy. If we could feed him to a bomb, we would."

What an astonishing thing for an astronaut to say about one of the architects of modern mission control! But however you look at it, the two versions of how the Apollo missions returned to Earth can't both be right! Someone's not telling the truth! At this point, two security guards removed Orbell from the room.

The Van Allen radiation belts

On several occasions journalist and Apollo sceptic Bart Sebril managed to bluff his way into the homes of a number of Apollo astronauts to conduct videotaped interviews with them. His true agenda soon became known and he was famously kicked by Edgar Mitchell, punched by Buzz Aldrin and subjected to dire threats by John Young!

Before his cover was blown, however he filmed some conversations that must make uncomfortable viewing for Apollo enthusiasts. Probably the most glaring contradiction he captured concerned the effect of the Van Allen radiation belts on astronauts passing through them.

These regions in near-Earth space consist of energetic charged particles held in place by the Earth's magnetic field: there are two ring doughnut-shaped belts that extend between 1,000 and 60,000 km from the Earth. The Apollo astronauts passed through the VA belts so rapidly that the even the thin aluminium skin of the Command Module was able to protect them from possible harmful effects. Several astronauts, however, reported experiencing frequent flashes in their eyes which, it was felt, might have been caused by charged particles striking the retina. This even occurred on a number of higher orbit Shuttle missions that circled the Earth well below the lower reaches of the Van Allen belts.

However, when Sibrel separately questioned Alan Bean and Gene Cernan about their experiences, the astronauts gave completely contradictory answers.

Capt Bean at first commented that he hadn't experienced any flashes or harmful effects but, curiously, then adds:

"I'm not sure we went far enough out to encounter the Van Allen radiation belts.... Maybe we did.... I don't know the distance to the VA belts! They hadn't been discovered yet."

(The Van Allen Belts were discovered in 1958 and had been the topic of frequent concerned discussion at NASA before the Moon landings)

Capt Cernan's recollection is entirely different: he states that the astronauts:

"... closed our eyes and put some light-sensitive pads on our eyes... we could see traces of radiation going through our eyes... we conducted this experiment several times, both going to the Moon and coming back from the Moon."

As Cernan answers Sibrel's politely-posed questions he begins to look extremely uncomfortable and begins to sweat copiously: it really does resemble the behaviour of a primed witness who can't quite remember what he is supposed to say!

There are many, many other strange discrepancies in the published accounts and photographic archives of the Apollo Program. Some of these are easily explained or are the result of poor research by people with little or no scientific background: however, some highly credible photographic analysts, aerospace engineers and diligent investigators have made a case that some or perhaps all the Apollo missions were elaborate hoaxes.

Just briefly, I want to return to Harrison Schmitt's comments (quoted earlier) about the damage inflicted on his and Gene Cernan's hands by the effort of bending their fingers inside the multi-layered EVA gloves. As I was browsing through images of the Apollo 17 mission, I came across a photo of the two Moonwalkers cutting a celebratory cake aboard the recovery vessel, the USS Ticonderoga. Their hands are spotless, with clean, manicured nails, completely at variance with Schmitt's memories. Moreover, Cernan has also stated:

"By the time the mission was all over, my hands were nothing but blisters. The skin on my knuckles was gone. Inside the glove, all the knuckle points were constantly scraping and, although they hurt, I guess I didn't let it bother me when we were on the surface. Your hands are so vital to everything you do that the gloves were custom fit; but we still ran into these problems."

There are many, many other strange discrepancies in the published accounts and photographic archives of the Apollo Program. Some of these are easily explained or are the result of poor research by people with little or no scientific background: however, some highly credible photographic analysts, aerospace engineers and diligent investigators have made a case that some or perhaps all the Apollo missions were elaborate hoaxes.

It is not the purpose of this book to examine all of these: rather, I hope the examples given above suggest that not everything in the space history books should be taken as a true record of events.

OUR FORBIDDEN MOON

CHAPTER 3:

A HIDDEN AGENDA

IF some or all of what is written above is true (and I believe that to be the case) several questions beg answers:

- How many astronauts – if any – actually visited the Moon?
- Supposing all six successful missions actually occurred, why are there so many discrepancies in the crews' accounts?
- Why were so many of the lunar surface photographs apparently faked?
- Why did the Moon missions abruptly cease after the return of Apollo 17 in 1972?
- Why, despite continued advances in IT and materials technology, have US, Russian and Chinese space missions been restricted to low Earth orbit?

After many years of research, and having spent time in conversation with over 30 astronauts (including at least one from each Gemini and Apollo mission from Apollo 7 to Apollo-Soyuz and Skylab!) I have reached the conclusion that as few as zero and as many as six men have walked on the lunar surface. But it is my contention that all of them – and most other astronauts and cosmonauts – are hiding an astonishing and possibly terrifying truth.

In my view, it is the need to sustain a shocking secret from the general public that is at the root of most, if not all, of the contradictions and discrepancies: it is also the reason why **authentic** lunar surface video and / or photography have not been made available and why since 1972 we as a species have been restricted to orbital missions just a few hundred kilometres above the Earth, with no plans to travel further in the foreseeable future. So just what might this 'shocking secret' be?

Let us consider these possibilities:

- The reality of the UFO phenomenon was known to NASA before manned spaceflight began in 1961.
- US & Soviet Astronauts expected to encounter EBEs and were prepared for the possibility.
- The presence of EBEs on the Moon was a factor in the cancellation of the final three Apollo missions.
- This factor continues to dictate current US spaceflight strategy.

It is generally conceded that the 'modern era' of interest in the UFO phenomenon began in 1947 with the sighting by pilot Kenneth Arnold of a flight of objects near Mt Rainier, Washington that he described as looking

"... like a saucer skipped across water"

It is believed by many that the same year a strange craft – with even stranger occupants – crashed near Roswell, New Mexico. There is a widespread conviction that much modern technology – and particularly that which allowed the development of novel aerospace alloys, hypersonic flight and microprocessors – was back-engineered from the crashed Roswell spacecraft or, perhaps, subsequently gifted to mankind by benevolent extraterrestrial beings.

The 'evidence' for the existence of the UFO phenomenon consists of literally tens of thousands of books, hundreds of hours of film and video and innumerable still photographs.

Even after seven decades of investigation and debate, the fundamental question remains unresolved: do UFOs exist and, if so, what exactly are they? Each of the many theories seems to explain one or more aspects of the phenomenon: setting aside deliberate hoaxing, these, and the main points they address, can be summarised as follows:

Natural or meteorological

This explains the absence of widely-acceptable physical evidence.

Inter-dimensional travel / time travel / worm-holes

These take into account the vast size of interstellar space and the velocity limits imposed by the General Theory of Relativity

Advanced human technology

The secrecy maintained by many governments and their apparent lack of interest in researching UFOs is understandable if they are their operators!

Hallucination & psychological pathology

All of the above, together with the abduction phenomenon and very close encounters, are explicable if we assume that the events occurred in the witnesses own minds.

There is also, of course, the explanation that was widely accepted at the start of the 'Flying Saucer' era: that UFOs are spacecraft operated by extra-terrestrial biological entities (EBEs)

To many people – particularly those who grew up during the heady years of the 'Space Age' between 1957 and 1972 – this seems by far the most logical and credible explanation: we were making our first stumbling steps into Space: surely the ultimate expression of this 'outward urge' would be to visit other star-systems and contact other intelligent life forms. If our species, then why not others?

But, ironically, it is the exploration of near-Earth space that has caused many people to doubt the extra-terrestrial hypothesis:

" If UFOs are spacecraft operated by alien astronauts, (the argument runs) *then why didn't our astronauts encounter them on the Moon or in Space?"*

So, in the final analysis, the 'ET Hypothesis' largely stands or falls upon this question: do US Astronauts and Soviet Cosmonauts believe in an extra-terrestrial origin for UFOs and have they encountered them during their missions? If the answer is 'No!' then it becomes almost impossible to support the 'alien spacecraft' identification.

The space travellers I have met, particularly those from the United States, are very patriotic. Although occasionally critical of the way some recent administrations have marginalised the space program, they generally support the official NASA line when discussing UFOs and other contentious issues in public. However, a few late-night sessions with a pitcher of margaritas or Tanqueray martinis have revealed some fascinating insights. The conclusion I have reached is that, during their missions many astronauts and cosmonauts have witnessed objects that defy immediate explanation. Since most of the pre-Shuttle spacemen have thousands of hours experience as test pilots or military aviators, it is perhaps unsurprising that a number have reported encountering UFOs in the atmosphere.

Pilots at the edge of space

Before anyone had ridden a rocket into space, an elite group of test pilots were 'pushing the outside of the envelope' in the astonishing North American X-15. Between September 1959 and October 1968, twelve aviators - including Neil Armstrong – flew as high as 67 miles above the Earth and as fast as 4,519 mph. Eight of these pilots were granted astronaut's wings, having flown above 50 miles altitude. Until 1958, it was planned to develop an orbital version of the craft, the X-15B.

NASA pilot Joseph Walker said that one of his tasks during his X-15 flights was to detect UFOs. He filmed five or six UFOs during his record breaking 50-mile-high flight in April, 1962, the second time he had done so. During a lecture at the Second National Conference on the Peaceful Uses of Space Research in Seattle, Washington he stated:

"I don't feel like speculating about them. All I know is what appeared on the film which was developed after the flight."

To date none of those films have been released for public viewing.

On July 17th, 1962 Major Robert White reported a UFO during his 58-mile high X-15 flight. Major White reported:

"I have no idea what it could be. It is greyish in colour and about thirty to forty feet away."

According to a Time Magazine article, Major White exclaimed over the radio:

"There ARE things out here! There absolutely are!"

But even before this, several pilots who would later fly into space as astronauts had their own other-worldly experiences. Donald 'Deke' Slayton was selected as a Mercury astronaut, became Head of the Astronaut Office and flew aboard the Apollo-Soyuz mission. Before his death in 1993, he told a reporter:

"I was testing a P-51 fighter in Minneapolis in 1951 when I spotted this

object. I was at about 10,000 feet on a nice, bright, sunny afternoon. I thought the object was a kite, then I realized that no kite is gonna fly that high.

As I got closer it looked like a weather balloon, gray and about three feet in diameter. But as soon as I got behind the darn thing it didn't look like a balloon anymore. It looked like a saucer, a disk.

About the same time, I realized that it was suddenly going away from me – and there I was running at about 300 miles per hour. I tracked it for a little way, and then all of a sudden the damn thing just took off. It pulled about a 45 degree climbing turn and accelerated and just flat disappeared."

Gordon Cooper, a fellow Mercury astronaut (who also orbited the Earth in a two-man Gemini spacecraft) was the last American to fly in space alone. It has been reported that he encountered a UFO on his Mercury-Atlas 9 mission, but he generally denied this in public. However, he most certainly would confirm that he witnessed several saucer-shaped aerial vehicles both from the cockpit of a plane and from the ground.

In a United Nations Debate on November 27, 1978, he stated:

"... several days in a row we sighted groups of metallic, saucer-shaped vehicles at great altitudes over the base [Germany, 1951] and we tried to get close to them; but they were able to change direction faster than our fighters. I do believe UFOs exist and that the truly unexplained ones are from some other technically advanced civilization."

Additionally, as a Project Manager at Edwards Airforce Base in 1958, Cooper assigned a group of men to film flight tests. They reported back to him that they had witnessed a circular object hovering over the strip, which landed briefly on retractable legs. It then flew off at incredible speed and at a sharp angle: not before they had exposed plenty of cine film, however!

This Cooper watched more than a dozen times before sending the only copy to Washington: needless to say, it disappeared!

Not long before his death, Cooper appeared on the popular Merv Griffin Show: in response to a question from Griffin about the Roswell Incident, he shocked everyone by stating:

"I think it's fairly credible. I would like to see the time when all qualified people could really work together to properly investigate these stories and either refute or prove them."

Cooper continued by saying that from the various reports he had seen, he was convinced that the occupants of this crashed UFO were:

"...probably not that different from what we are: that they are almost totally humanoid in appearance, have two arms, two legs, a torso and readily identifiable facial features."

Of these early astronauts, one of the most intriguing was M Scott Carpenter, the second American to orbit the Earth. Like several others after him, Carpenter fell foul of Flight Director Chris Kraft, who had him removed from the spaceflight roster. I was fortunate enough to be able to chat with him on three occasions: once we sat together at a major autograph show for a whole weekend. I asked him if it were true that he had reportedly stated:

"At no time, when our astronauts are in space are they alone: there is a constant surveillance by UFOs."

Carpenter confirmed that he had indeed said

"...something like that: my personal knowledge is from Mercury, but I believe this continues to be the case."

I asked if he was referring to the 'fire-flies' that he and John Glenn had observed during their Mercury missions: these he dismissed as ice crystals or frozen urine

Two up! The Gemini Program

As an essential precursor to a manned landing on the Moon, American astronauts needed to acquire the skills of orbital rendezvous and docking. Additionally, much of the equipment and many of the techniques associated with EVA and long duration spaceflight had to be developed and tested. During 1965 and 1966, a total of sixteen astronauts flew ten missions, accomplishing all the Program's aims. (Although not without some near-disasters)

Most of the Gemini Astronauts were chosen to train for missions to the Moon, and several have been forthcoming with accounts of unknown objects encountered in low Earth orbit. Almost all of the others are widely reported as having had similar experiences, but always have refrained from public discussion: this could have been out of a fear of being dropped from the flight roster.

Gen James McDivitt, Gemini IV, Apollo 9

During his Gemini IV mission in 1965, Gen James McDivitt, witnessed an apparently metallic cylinder with antenna-like structures, which he attempted to photograph.

On the first of two occasions when we met (and enjoyed a jug of margaritas together!) I asked why he hadn't woken his fellow crew-member, Edward White. He replied that:

"...it wasn't in the mission profile. I was on watch, Ed was scheduled for a sleep period. You have to understand the military way of things: you do what's in the profile!"

Later, however, both astronauts reported two egg-shaped objects leaving glowing trails. McDivitt told me that the photographs of these on many websites are either fakes or merely show reflections in Gemini IV's window: he has never seen prints of the exposures he made, and feels it is likely they were over exposed due to the UFO's proximity to the Sun. He is, however, adamant that these objects were artificial structures that bore no resemblance to any US or Soviet spacecraft Capt.

James Lovell, Gemini VII & XII, Apollo 8 &13

I have met Capt James Lovell on several occasions and had the opportunity to ask about the 'bogies' that were reported on his Gemini VII mission. (The word 'bogie' is used by military pilots for any unknown and potentially, hostile aircraft) He stands by his original statement that he and Col. Frank Borman were not looking at the top stage of their Titan II launch vehicle, which they could distantly see at the same time. He also confirmed that he and Buzz Aldrin observed four 'bright unknowns' during their Gemini XII mission, but considers that these could have been

"...bags of trash we threw out earlier!"

Capt Lovell laughs at the interpretation of his well-known Apollo 8 communication about seeing Santa Claus, remarking that the tongue-in-cheek comment was, after all, made on Christmas Day.

Capt. Gene Cernan: Gemini IX, Apollo 10 & 17

When asked to confirm widely reported sightings of UFOs during his three space missions, Cernan (paraphrasing his widely-published quote) said:

"Look: I've already told people that I believe they (UFOs) *are real and that they come from someplace else: from some other technological civilization. There is too much evidence not to* (believe that)*"*

He was, however, not prepared to admit publicly that he had any personal experience of the UFO phenomenon: however, later on I will examine a very curious photograph he took during his Apollo 17 Moon mission.

OUR FORBIDDEN MOON

Capt. Richard Gordon: Gemini XI, Apollo 12

I have twice met Capt. Gordon, sitting with him at the dinner table for three hours on one occasion! I asked him about the reported encounter with a UFO during the Gemini XI mission. He confirmed that both he and Pete Conrad had seen a bright object, which Conrad had photographed. Gordon stated that this had subsequently been identified by NASA as the Soviet Proton 3 satellite: he felt this was unlikely, since the object had visible length, which would not have been the case with a 3 metre long spacecraft 450 km away.

To the Moon and back.... The Apollo missions

The Apollo Program was, to outward appearances, an ingenious and successful response to President John Kennedy's 1961 pledge that an American would walk on the Moon by the end of the decade. Using, at the time, the largest booster rockets ever built, the modular Apollo Spacecraft was launched into Earth orbit. Following a TLI (trans-lunar injection) rocket firing, the complete spacecraft then left Earth orbit and travelled towards the Moon. The Command and Service Modules were separated from the top (S-IVB) stage of the Saturn launch rocket, turned around and docked with the spider-like Lunar Module. The Apollo 'stack' then pulled away from the S-IVB stage, which entered solar orbit. After 2-3 days, the spacecraft achieved lunar orbit by a deceleration 'burn' that dramatically took place behind the Moon. Once in lunar orbit, the LM was checked, separated, and its four landing legs deployed.

The tense journey to the Moon's surface was initiated by a firing of to plan, the LM reached its chosen landing site about a quarter of an hour later. The two Moonwalker astronauts then carried out an exploration of the surrounding surface (which increased with each mission to a total of over 22 hours EVA on Apollo 17) Following the setting up of experimental packages

OUR FORBIDDEN MOON

The red circle around the Earth indicates to scale the height of an average Shuttle mission
The diagram below shows the Earth-Moon system to scale

Earth · — 380,000 km — · Moon

and the collection of rock and regolith samples, the Moonwalkers returned to the LM for the final time, fired the ascent stage motor and rendezvoused with the CM in lunar orbit. The return to Earth was then accomplished in a near-reverse process of the outward journey. Simple!

The internet is awash with chilling accounts of how the Apollo Astronauts encountered UFOs before, during and after their lunar EVAs, but the vast majority of these are simply fiction. That isn't to say that there were no such encounters: rather that if they did take place they do not form part of the public record.

However, as they grow older and less constrained by duty, patriotism and, perhaps, fear of ridicule, some of the Apollo crewmen have begun to hint that there is something incredible that they haven't yet disclosed.

Perhaps it is having to keep an earth-shattering secret for more than fifty years that explains the strange behaviour of many of the astronauts, or perhaps it is simply a case of "When you've been to the Moon, what else is there to do?" Whichever, it is at least a little interesting to review the post-Apollo careers of the twelve Moonwalkers.

Neil Armstrong, Gemini X, Apollo 11

It is frequently claimed that Armstrong became some kind of recluse following his historic first landing at Tranquillity Base in 1969. This is far from the truth: in the months following his return from the Moon he took part in a goodwill tour, attending public functions around the World, making countless speeches, giving interviews on radio & TV and signing literally hundreds of thousands of autographs. (Notwithstanding this, autographed photographs of Armstrong in his white spacesuit still fetch over £1000 in online auctions!

Having announced that he would not participate in any further space missions, Armstrong accepted a post as Deputy Associate Administrator for aeronautics for the Office of Advanced Research and Technology, Advanced Research Projects Agency. After a year he left NASA to take up the role of Professor of Aerospace Engineering at Cincinnati University. Following an eight year tenure, Armstrong resigned, filling his time on a range of pursuits: working on his farm, serving on Boards of Directors attending airshows and other public events. He stopped signing autographs in 1994, irritated by the huge sums his signature was sold for, by people to whom he had given it so freely

But Armstrong did say a few strange things that deserve closer examination.

At their first post-flight press conference (a video of which is widely available online) the Apollo 11 astronauts seem oddly subdued and ill at ease. NASA enthusiasts have explained their behaviour as being caused by understandable discomfort at becoming instant celebrities. But is this credible? All three men had flown on previous missions and been fêted afterwards: Armstrong was a decorated hero of the Korean War and one of the elite X-15 test pilots. Following his Gemini X mission, Armstrong and his wife took part in a 24-day goodwill tour of South America, visiting 11 countries and 14 major cities, even making addresses in foreign languages and dialects!

I once showed the press conference video to a leading Clinical Psychologist. He had no real interest in space travel and failed to recognize the three astronauts: I had the sound turned off, so he had just the men's body language and facial expressions to consider. His opinion was that:

"...the man in the middle (Armstrong) *is not telling the truth: the hand movements and averted gaze of the other two men are typical of dissociation'*

Additionally, Armstrong says a few strange things during the press conference, possibly the most interesting being during his opening comments:

"It was our privilege to have participated in one great adventure. It was an adventure that took place... not ....just in the month of July...."

There is an obvious pause after the word 'not': those of us who enjoy watching American TV programs will be familiar with this form of irony. (eg: 'That's a great haircut: NOT!')

It is almost as if Armstrong is intimating that the mission didn't take place! He made a similarly cryptic comment in 1994, when addressing a group of students at the White House. He tells his audience that what the US had achieved in Space at that point was just a first step, with much still left to be done, before suddenly becoming quite emotional – almost tearful – and commenting

"...breakthroughs are available to those who can remove one of truth's protective layers."

It should be borne in mind that this choice of words was quite deliberate: Armstrong was reading from prepared notes.

Armstrong's private life was both tragic and, at times, turbulent: perhaps there may have been times when he regretted putting himself forward for selection as an astronaut. However, none of this fully explains the curious ambiguity of some of his public reflections about the Moon landings, nor the often emotional way in which they were delivered. At the time – and subsequently – I felt that 'mankind's first visitor to another world' had a secret he desperately wished he could share.

It is generally considered that the reason for scattering Armstrong's ashes at sea (subsequent to his death following heart by-pass surgery) was to prevent ghoulish collectors from desecrating a grave-site. For the sake of completeness, I would just mention that other commentators have wondered whether Armstrong was thought to be getting close to some form of disclosure and that his possibly convenient demise was followed by the irretrievable disposal of his remains.

OUR FORBIDDEN MOON

Dr Buzz Aldrin, Gemini XII, Apollo 11

Of the fourteen Apollo astronauts I have met, I have to say that Buzz Aldrin is the one I found least easy to warm to. History records that, following a glittering career as a military aviator and test pilot, he was the second man to walk on the Moon. Yet on the three occasions I have spent time in his company, I saw little of the good humour and modesty that typified the other Apollo astronauts.

Nevertheless, there has been no shortage of attendees at autograph shows willing to pay up to £375 for Dr Aldrin's signature or nearly double that for adding his name to an item already signed by CM Pilot Michael Collins!

Given his worldwide celebrity, one of the things I find most curious about Dr Aldrin is the way he exaggerates his importance within the astronaut corps and to the Apollo 11 mission: here are some facts capable of being verified online:

- So unpopular was Aldrin among the astronauts that Armstrong was given the opportunity to replace him with James Lovell as LM Pilot.

- The LM Pilot was considered to be third in crew seniority order: the main reason Armstrong declined the substitution was because he didn't want to affect Lovell's future selection as a mission commander by agreeing to what was effectively a demotion.

- Aldrin claims that he solved the problem of a broken engine-arm circuit breaker. (Reluctantly accepting blame for having broken it himself!) In his account, failure to come up with a way to operate the circuit breaker would have marooned the astronauts on the lunar surface. Here's his version:

- *"As I got down on the floor to sleep, I could see the broken head of a circuit breaker. It was the engine-arm circuit breaker--the one that's got to be in to get electricity to turn the ascent engine on. Since it was on my side, obviously I would have to take the blame for my backpack knocking against things clumsily and breaking it off."*

Here's the less dramatic truth from Hal Loden, the Lunar Module Control Officer:

"That circuit breaker allowed the lunar guidance system to start the engine automatically, but there was another way to start the engine. We had redundancy. They would have had to hit a pushbutton manually at T minus zero."

Aldrin continues to claim that he pushed in the stub of the button with a pen.

- Aldrin has always presented as being bitter about not being first on the Moon: he claims that precedent set during Gemini was for the junior crew member to conduct the first EVA, and seems to have believed that Armstrong got the nod because NASA wanted a civilian to be first out of the door. Chris Kraft, head of Mission Control for the Apollo missions, wrote in his memoir *'Flight'* :

"Buzz Aldrin desperately wanted that honor and wasn't quiet in letting it be known."

In fact, there was never the slightest chance of Aldrin being first down the ladder: as a Group 2 Astronaut, and mission commander, Armstrong had seniority over Aldrin and, more importantly, the design of the LM hatch made it virtually impossible for the LMP to leave until the commander had exited.

- There are lots of plausible explanations as to why there are no posed stills photographs of Armstrong on the surface: these include time constraints, President Nixon wanting to talk to the astronauts as they were about to swap over the camera and, as Aldrin tells it, Armstrong was given use of the camera for most of the EVA to take 'technical' photographs. However, there remains the lingering thought that Aldrin may have conveniently not noticed opportunities to take the camera from Armstrong!

At an autograph show I once attended, Dr Aldrin was asked to write something different to the usual quotes and platitudes. To everyone's amazement, he added:

'Walking on the Moon is like making love – being first doesn't mean you were best!'

Dr Aldrin has frequently hinted that we might not be alone in the Universe: this belief is central to the plots of his two novels 'Encounter with Tiber' and 'The Return'.

More recently, he has claimed that an apparently artificial structure has been discovered on Phobos, one of the two small satellites of Mars. In an interview with C-Span, an American cable network news station, Aldrin stated:

"We should visit the moon of Mars. There is a monolith there, a very unusual structure on this little potato-shaped object that goes around Mars."

Perhaps better-known is Aldrin's account of a UFO following the Apollo stack out of Earth orbit. In his first discussion of the object, he was adamant that it was not the S-IVB upper stage, which was too far away to be visible. He has said several times that the crew decided to ignore it, because of the danger that NASA might abort the mission! These days, however, Aldrin has accepted the official line that the object was one of the petal-like covers that protected the LM during launch. He has categorically stated that *all* the photos purporting to be of the object are crude fakes.

Capt. Charles 'Pete' Conrad, Gemini V & XI, Apollo 12, Skylab 2

Of all the Apollo Astronauts, Conrad is the one I most regret not having the chance to meet!

If you've ever seen the film 'The Right Stuff' (which, by the way, most astronauts seem to hate!) you'll remember that Gordon Cooper is occasionally asked

"Who's the best pilot you ever saw?"

to which he replies

"You're looking at him, kid!"

In fact, I was told by fellow Apollo 12 astronaut Richard Gordon that this was actually Pete Conrad's line! I assume Conrad's senior position in the astronaut corps wasn't highlighted in the film because Conrad was already dead by the time it was made, killed in a motorcycle accident on a straight road with no-one else involved.

In 2014, I had the chance to spend an hour chatting to Rick Armstrong, the Apollo 11 Moonwalker's elder son. He told me some hilarious anecdotes about his father's friendship with Conrad and the vacations the two families spent together on the Armstrong's ranch. This conversation confirmed both Conrad's legendary sense of humour and the independence of his spirit.

Conrad failed the Group 1 astronaut selection test because of his frustration with the apparent pointlessness of some of the procedures. At one point he was asked to provide a stool sample for testing: this he delivered in a gift box tied with a ribbon! His final act was to drop a full enema bag on the medical director's desk before walking out of the selection process. It is said that fellow Naval Pilot Alan Shepard persuaded Conrad to reapply for astronaut status: he was successful, joining Armstrong, McDivitt, Lovell,

OUR FORBIDDEN MOON

Young, Stafford, Borman, See and White in Group 2. (Both White and See were killed before they could undertake an Apollo mission, as were Group 3 astronauts Bassett, Chaffee, Freeman and Williams)

Conrad would need his resourcefulness and intelligence as Commander of Apollo 12: there are several features of the Apollo 12 mission that almost seem too good - or bad - to be true!

Firstly, it is claimed that the Saturn V launch vehicle was twice struck by lightning shortly after liftoff, causing an instrumentation problem that seemed to suggest that the spacecraft's power system had failed. Fortunately the mission EECOM, John Aaron, remembered a similar situation during a simulation exercise and made the correct call to Flight Director Gerry Griffin. Griffin was expecting Aaron to advise a mission abort and admitted to me that he didn't initially understand his 'SCE to AUX' call.

I asked Griffin about the lightning strike and the various wild accounts about it that have appeared online and in print. He admitted that it was only when film of the launch was examined later that frames appearing to show an electrical discharge from the Saturn rocket's exhaust plume and the launch tower were discovered. He, and the control team, was, he said, responding to an alert that suggested that the CM electrical buss had failed.

Perhaps surprisingly, two of the three astronauts – Gordon, the CM Pilot and Conrad, the Mission Commander - couldn't recall the location of the switch that needed resetting. Fortunately Alan Bean, the rookie with no space flight experience, instantly reset the 'signal conditioning equipment' switch to 'auxiliary', saving the mission.

A second amazing detail of the Apollo 12 mission is how close the LM landed to the Surveyor 3 spacecraft. This had soft-landed in the Mare Cognitum region of the Oceanus Procellarum ('Ocean of Storms') in April 1967. Considering the problems Armstrong had experienced in finding a suitable landing site (almost, we are told, running out of fuel for the descent stage in the attempt) this was an amazing piece of flying – or luck! Pieces of the spacecraft were detached and returned to Earth to evaluate the 'possibility of interplanetary contamination' It is widely claimed that terrestrial bacteria were discovered on subsequent examination, but many authorities have questioned this. But you have to ask: why limit the amount of rocks that could be brought back by the mission and compromise EVA time to retrieve chunks of Surveyor 3? Couldn't Conrad and Bean simply have obtained swabs for testing? A cynic might suggest that the apparent return to Earth of pieces of a spacecraft that indisputably landed on the Moon is a good way to prove that astronauts were there to do the job!

Capt. Alan Bean, Apollo 12, Skylab 3

Capt. Alan Bean was a kind, reflective man: when I first met him, he reminded me of one of those old guys who sits on a sunlit bench outside a country pub telling stories of the good old days! He devoted much of his time after his retirement as an astronaut in producing very competent impasto oil paintings of the US space program. On one occasion he was even kind enough to offer praise for some of my artistic efforts: he was, as I said above a very kind person!

Capt. Bean's very selection for the Apollo 12 crew raises a few questions. He had no spaceflight experience, failed to pass selection for Group 2 and was not particularly prominent among the rest of the astronaut corps. He had been slotted into the Apollo Applications Program, which was tasked with investigating and training for spaceflight options after the final Apollo mission

When Clifton Williams (backup astronaut for the Apollo 9 mission) was killed in an air crash, Bean's instructor at test pilot school, Pete Conrad, personally intervened in his selection as replacement. One wonders what

OUR FORBIDDEN MOON

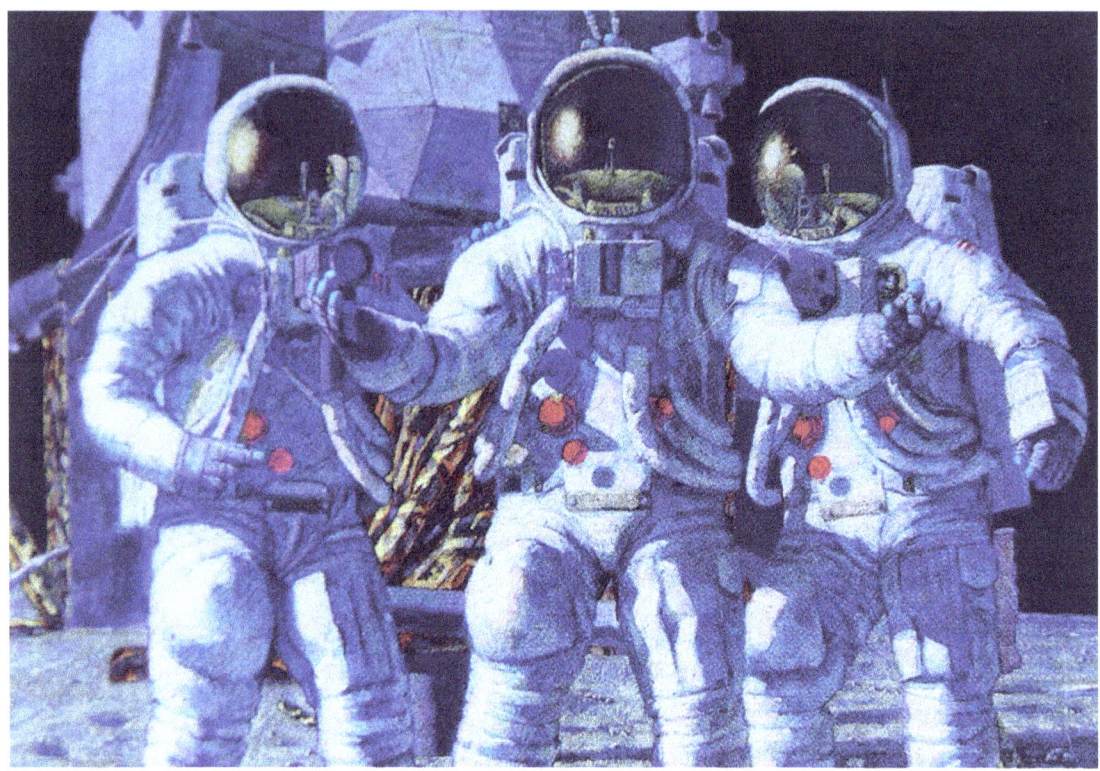

other Group 1, 2 & 3 astronauts who weren't so lucky thought about Bean's promotion up the flight order.

Bean committed an almost unforgivable act on the initial Apollo 12 EVA: almost the first thing he was tasked to do was prepare the colour television camera. Unaccountably, we are told that he pointed it at the Sun, irreparably damaging it and precluding any live TV feed from the mission. (Very convenient, some might say!) Strangely, if you watch the online record of this event, it actually seems as if Capt Bean in fact swivelled the camera downwards to point into shadow: it appears to continue transmitting a very dark, blurred image for some time after it was allegedly destroyed.

On one of the two occasions I spoke with him, Capt Bean told me that he and Conrad had planned a practical joke on the mission controllers. They had intended to use a self-timer on the Hasselblad stills camera to photograph both Moonwalkers together by the side of the Surveyor 3 spacecraft. This would, of course, have begged the question as to who was pressing the shutter! In the event, neither astronaut could locate the device in the tool carrier tote bag. This seems strange: they presumably had time to look for it on the way to the Moon! Was this photograph really just intended to be a bit of fun or

"...a wonderful memory of our time on the surface together"

as Bean recalled during a conversation I had with him in 2014.

Perhaps this anecdote should be considered alongside one of Capt Bean's paintings, **'The Fantasy'**.

Bean is particularly fond of this piece of artwork: he has used it as the cover of one of his books and as his business card. It depicts an EVA on the lunar surface, but, curiously shows all three Apollo 12 astronauts, including CM Pilot Richard Gordon! Is Bean merely creating an image of a reality he wished had taken place? Or is the title of the piece hinting at a darker truth?

On 28th July, 1973, Bean commanded the second mission to Skylab. This, America's first manned space station, was a product of the Apollo Applications Program, which Capt. Bean had worked on before selection for Apollo 12. Before an anticipated but uncontrolled re-entry in January, 1975, Skylab had hosted three manned missions and achieved many of its stated aims.

During the Skylab 3 mission, the three-man Crew of Bean, Garriott and Lousma witnessed a much-discussed encounter with a UFO, which was photographed and kept under observation for over ten minutes. The astronauts discussed the encounter with CAPCOM shortly afterwards:

Lousma: *Did you tell him about that satellite we saw?*

OUR FORBIDDEN MOON

Bean: *Yes, we saw a great satellite. We didn't know if we told you about it.*

Lousma: *The closest and brightest one we've seen.*

Bean: *Huge one!*

Lousma: *We've seen several. It was a red one.*

Capsule Communicator: *No, you may have told someone but it wasn't this team. I don't remember hearing about it.*

Lousma: *I guess we didn't report it. It was reflecting in red light and oscillating at, oh, counting its period of brightness to dimmest, about 10 seconds. It led us into sunset. That was about three revs ago, I think. Something like that, wasn't it Owen?* (No answer).

During debriefing on 4th October, following their return to Earth, the incident was discussed again. The mere fact that they again brought up the encounter suggests that the astronauts had seen more than just the tiny piece of debris or conventional satellites suggested as possible identifications by several 'debunker' websites:

Garriott: *Do you want to talk about that satellite?*

Lousma: *I saw a couple of satellites that appeared like a satellite would on Earth. I saw one that was not like one you would see on Earth, so why don't you mention it.*

Garriott: *OK. About a week or 10 days before recovery and we were still waiting for information to be supplied to us about the identification. Jack first notices this rather large red star out the wardroom window. Upon close examination, it was much brighter than Jupiter or any of the other planets. It had a reddish hue to it, even though it was well above the horizon. The light from the Sun was not passing close to the Earth's limb at the time. We observed it for about 10 minutes prior to sunset. It was slowly rotating because it had a variation in brightness with a 10-seconds period. As I was saying, we observed it for about 10 minutes, until we went into darkness, and it also followed us into darkness about 5-seconds later. From the 5 to 10 second delay in its disappearance we surmised that it was not more than 30 to 50 nautical miles (35 to 58 statute miles or 56 to 93 km) from our location. From its original position in the wardroom window, it did not move more than 10 or 20 degrees over the 10 minutes or so that we watched it. Its orbit was very close to that of our own. We never saw it on any earlier or succeeding orbits and we'd be quite interested in having its identification established. It's all debriefed in terms of time on channel A, so the precise timing and location can be picked up from there.*

I have met both Capt Bean and Col Lousma and have briefly discussed the incident with both men. They had little to add, other than to confirm the general accuracy of the account and of the following rendition of the object:

Admiral Alan Shepard, Mercury MR-3, Apollo 14

My reason for reviewing the activities of the twelve Moonwalkers before, during and after the defining missions of their time in the astronaut corps is, you will recall, to consider whether this can help explain America's abrupt termination of the Apollo program in 1972 and subsequent failure to send manned spacecraft beyond low Earth orbit.

In this respect, almost nothing is more bizarre than Admiral Shepard's career!

In this age where little or no astronomy or modern history seem to be taught in English schools, I find it astonishing how few people are aware that Alan Shepard was the first American to fly in space: far more remember Soviet Cosmonaut Yuri Gagarin. The reason for this could possibly be that his historic flight took place long ago in 1961, but more probably it's because

OUR FORBIDDEN MOON

his Mercury-Redstone MR-3 mission was little more than a ballistic hop to the edge of the atmosphere, lasting just fifteen minutes.

Shepard, despite his seniority and prestige, never flew a Gemini mission: this should have totally precluded his selection for the Apollo Program. Shepard was removed from the flight roster for five years (1964–69) when he was found to be suffering from Ménière's disease, a disorientating disease of the inner-ear. During this time, and following his Apollo mission, Shepard served as Head of the Astronaut Office. At a cocktail party, he allegedly heard of a surgical procedure to correct the condition, which he discussed with fellow Mercury astronaut, friend and Director of Flight Crew Operations, Donald 'Deke' Slayton. Incredibly, despite his lack of recent experience, Shepard was slotted into the program as Commander of Apollo 14, advancing to Apollo 13 the named crew of James Lovell, Ken Mattingly, and Fred Haise! Even more astonishingly, his two crew-mates, Dr Edgar Mitchell and Col. Stuart Roosa (although both exceptional pilots) were total space rookies!

An uncommitted reader presented with these facts might, perhaps, wonder whether the Apollo 14 mission ever took place, especially if he then went on to consider the actions of the mission's two Moonwalkers.

Most space-geeks are aware that Shepard smuggled the head of a six-iron golf club and some golf balls onto the LM. Using the handle of a lunar excavation tool as a shaft, he hit two golf shots with limited success, the furthest probably travelling just 200m. Mitchell's contribution to sports day was to throw a lunar scoop handle as if it were a javelin! As we will see below, Mitchell went on to conduct his own unauthorised paranormal researches on the Moon. Whether this attempted telepathy or unscheduled sporting activities had any effect is a moot point, but is a fact that some of the mission tasks were uncompleted. The two astronauts, pulling behind

OUR FORBIDDEN MOON

them a Mobile Equipment Transporter (MET) were tasked to climb to the rim of Cone Crater: this they failed to do, stopping 30m short.

Later, Shepard used his position in the Astronaut Office to return his old friend Slayton's favour, helping him return to flight status in time to command the Apollo Soyuz Test Project. (Slayton had been removed from active status during the Mercury Program when he was found to be suffering from a heart murmur.)

Dr Edgar Mitchell, Apollo 14

I met Dr Mitchell a number of times and have discussed both his Apollo 14 mission and the UFO phenomenon with him. He famously grew up close to Roswell, NM, which may account for his open-minded attitude to the UFO phenomenon in particular and parascience in general.

Without NASA's knowledge, Dr Mitchell conducted an ESP experiment with four subjects back on Earth. They tried to guess the correct order of some standard symbols as he attempted to project them telepathically: Mitchell describes the experiment as

"...moderately successful"

In an interview with journalist Steve McNamara, Mitchell has described a strange experience he underwent during his return from the Moon:

"The really profound experience came on the way back. And that really didn't have anything to do with parapsychology. I only later started to see the tie-in. Up to that time my parapsychology was simply an intellectual search for avenues of knowledge. What happened on the way back happened fairly quickly. It was a field consciousness experience. There's a range of consciousness open to human beings and it goes from material consciousness at one end to what we call field consciousness.

A person feels at one with the universe, perceiving the universe. I think

that's probably the way Jim Irwin felt when he said he felt he was in the presence of God. All of a sudden it was, "Hey, there's something I'm feeling that's different," It's not a cumulative awareness of any sort. It is a sudden change of consciousness state."

Over drinks in October 2011, Dr Mitchell amazed several friends and me by casually mentioning that he had been briefed that US intelligence agencies are actively working with four alien species, which he went on to describe. I asked if he would include this information in the next day's lecture: he agreed and did so! Despite a good measure of incredulity – and even hostility – from the audience, Dr Mitchell reiterated his claims and went on to confirm his belief in the broad truth of the Roswell incident.

I mentioned Dr Mitchell's name in correspondence with Jesse Marcel, Jnr, son of the famous (or notorious!) Air Intelligence Officer at Roswell: he was kind enough to send me a signed copy of his own book and suggested that Dr Mitchell's interest in spaceflight and the UFO phenomenon were possibly kindled by his childhood experiences and memories of the Roswell Incident.

Col. David Scott, Gemini VIII, Apollo 9 & 15

Col Scott was, for many years, the quiet man of the Apollo Program. His 'comic book hero' good looks, extraordinary courage and resourcefulness on the near-disastrous Gemini VIII mission and his exemplary conduct on his two Apollo missions were marred, according to many commentators, by a curious lack of judgement during the preparations for Apollo 15. Apparently following urging by Deke Slayton, Scott made a secret deal with Hermann Sieger, a German stamp dealer. In addition to the 243 authorised commemorative 'covers' carried aboard Apollo 15, an additional 398 were flown to the Moon: 100 of these were given to Sieger as his 'cut'. When these appeared on the open market, Congress demanded a NASA investigation, which ultimately resulted in Scott and his Apollo 15 crewmates Irwin &

OUR FORBIDDEN MOON

Worden being disciplined: none of the three ever flew in Space again. In fact, the Apollo 15 crew's actions were not specifically forbidden by NASA and it was a well-established practice that astronauts could and would make some provision for their families in the event of a catastrophic end to their mission.

Among the most sought-after items of memorabilia are the so-called 'Insurance Covers', stamped and franked envelopes signed by all three crew members of each mission. In most cases, these were offered for sale almost as soon as the astronauts returned to Earth. The same is true of commemorative medallions containing a tiny fraction of silver from a flown-to-the-Moon item. Scott's reputation was further tarnished when he left his wife of over 40 years to begin a much-publicised relationship with TV

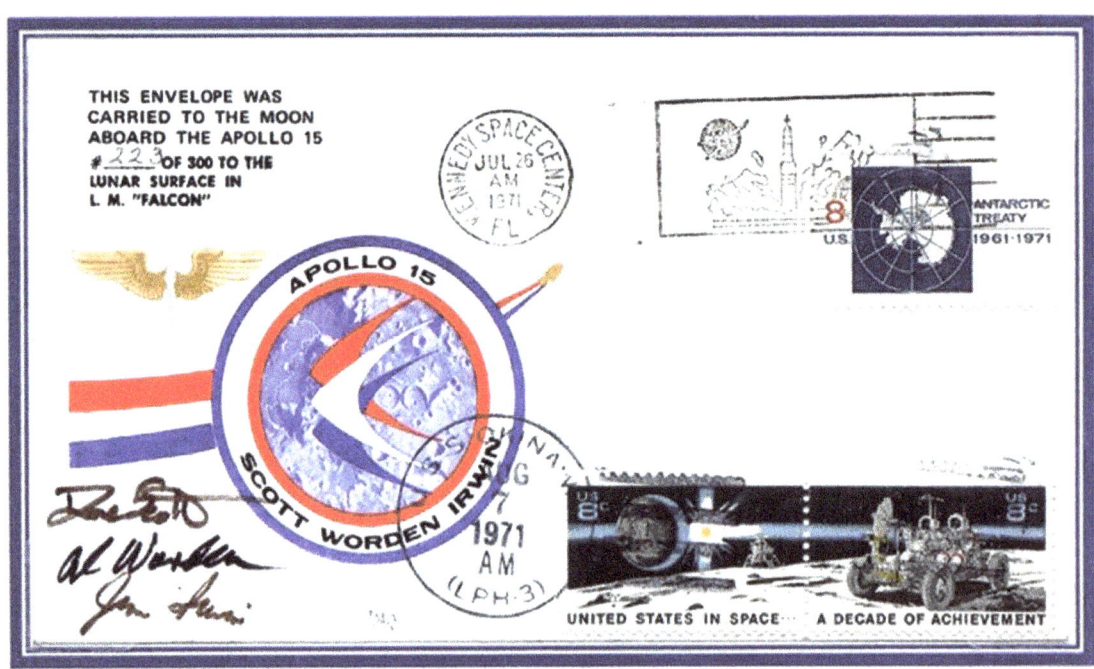

Apollo 15 'Sieger Cover'

Col. & Mrs Scott, Mr & Mrs Bryant

personality Anna Ford. (As an aside, it is interesting how many marriages the twelve 'Moonwalkers' have logged between them: Aldrin and Mitchell three, Armstrong, Bean, Cernan, Scott, Conrad & Young two each)

I have met Col. Scott on two occasions and found him a good-natured and amiable man, as long as the conversation was kept light!

Col. James Irwin, Apollo 15

Lunar Module Pilot on Apollo 15, Jim Irwin was a spaceflight rookie on this, his only mission. Of the twelve astronauts who allegedly walked on the Moon, three apparently experienced powerful epiphanies that changed their lives completely: of these, the most dramatic seems to have been Irwin's.

During his time on the lunar surface, Irwin's heart rhythms began to show signs of irregularity. This potentially critical condition was ameliorated by zero gravity on the return to Earth and a pure oxygen environment in the Command Module: however, a few months later Irwin suffered a heart attack. This, and his involvement with the Sieger stamp controversy, led to him leaving the Air Force and NASA in 1972, whereupon he founded the 'High Flight Foundation', an evangelical Christian organisation. Irwin spent the remaining twenty years of his life as 'A goodwill ambassador for the Prince of Peace', writing books, pamphlets and giving talks about how his experiences on the Moon had made

> *"....the presence of God real* (to him)*"*

In 1973, Irwin embarked on what, to many people, seemed an incredibly bizarre new mission: to discover Noah's Ark on Mount Ararat. A belief in the possibility of discovering the actual Ark built by Noah before the biblical flood described in Chapters 6 – 9 of the Book of Genesis seems, to say the least, a little strange for a highly trained pilot and geologist like Irwin. He took part in several expeditions to the mountain, on one occasion experiencing a severe fall which necessitated him being carried down the mountain for evacuation to hospital.

Perhaps not unconnected to this, Irwin suffered at least two more heart attacks before dying in 1991, the first Moonwalker to do so.

Capt. John Young, Gemini III & X, Apollo 10 & 16, STS-1 & 9

John Young appears at first sight to have been the quintessential space hero: handsome, brave, modest and hugely experienced (He was a member of the first Gemini Crew, flew to the Moon twice and commanded the first Space Shuttle mission.) Set against this, however, was an apparent reluctance to discuss his experiences in print, in interviews or at personal appearances. He customarily stated that he was paid by the Navy and would refuse invitations

OUR FORBIDDEN MOON

to take part in such events until he retired. When eventually he did leave NASA in 2004, he finally wrote an autobiography, somewhat strangely titled 'Forever Young'. This book has a number of perplexing factual errors, not the least hard to understand being that Young describes the Lunar Module as having three legs!

Had he really forgotten such a basic detail of his spacecraft, or was he trying to hint at something?

Gen. Charles Duke, Apollo 16

Unlike Col. Irwin and Dr Mitchell, Gen. Duke's time on the Moon does not seem to have affected him spiritually. By his own account, the stress of life as an ex-Moonwalker and a growing dependence on alcohol caused problems in both his family and professional life and it was only through the intervention of his wife's Minister and Duke's Christian 'rebirth' that his marriage was saved.

There are many curious inconsistencies in Gen. Duke's recollections of the Apollo 16 mission, not least his insistence that stars cannot be seen from the lunar surface or in cis-lunar space.

Stars were reportedly photographed several times on various missions and the planet Venus was apparently captured on an image – AS14-64-9191 – taken on the Moon by Admiral Shepard: it is the bright 'star' just to the right of the dish antenna.

NASA can't have it both ways! Either the stars couldn't be seen or photographed or they could! The Shepard photograph is explained as being the result of the brightness of Venus when seen from an airless world: but this would also be the case for the brighter stars such as Sirius, Arcturus, Canopus, Vega and so on. But NASA PR men have frequently stated that the exposure and aperture settings of the mission stills cameras would not allow any images of objects less bright in the lunar sky than the Earth and Sun!

OUR FORBIDDEN MOON

Venus, seen from the Moon (Apollo 14)

Some commentators have suggested that Gen. Duke's commitment to evangelical Christianity owes more to battling his personal demons than to a spiritual epiphany while on the Moon. At times he almost seems to use his faith as a shield during controversial debate.

Capt. Gene Cernan, Gemini IXA, Apollo 10 & 17

Capt. Cernan seems to deviate more than any other Moonwalker from the accepted 'Right Stuff' profile of an astronaut, both in his behaviour before and during the Apollo 17 mission and in his subsequent public pronouncements. I have met him on two occasions and was astonished how ready he was to attack the reputations off his fellow Apollo astronauts, particularly Buzz Aldrin. He was also extremely critical of recent US presidents and their failure to support manned lunar and Martian expeditions.

Cernan's behaviour in the run up to the Apollo 17 mission reads like a B-movie film script: it stretches the credibility of all but the most avid Apollo enthusiast. Firstly, it was discovered in a routine check that Cernan had a prostate infection: the following is his own account from his autobiography:

"Chuck La Pinta, our Apollo 17 flight surgeon and a good guy, was poking around my body during a physical exam and discovered I had a prostate infection.

Chuck was a medical anomaly, so he didn't run out, ring bells, alarm everybody, and report me as being unfit. Instead he told no one at all, but worked quietly to resolve the problem. 'We'll take care of it here,' my nonchalant doctor said with a deadpan expression, humourless eyes watching below the brim of the porkpie hat he always wore. I gladly agreed to be treated in secret, because I didn't want some manager to think I was anything less than a genuine, totally healthy astronaut."

How extraordinary! By his own admission, Cernan conspired with a NASA official to conceal a potentially mission-compromising condition!

Astonishingly, more was to come! Shortly after Cernan began his regime of prostate massage with Dr La Pinta, he elected to take part in an energetic game of softball. He hit a line drive and began running:

"I could almost hear something snap inside my leg as I rounded second base. It felt like a machete had chopped deep into my lower calf, and I hit the dirt with a roll and a scream of agony. Within sight of my Saturn rocket, and watched by most of our launch team, a tendon in my right leg had given way, and I lay there with my brain storming. Goddamn, what have I done?"

Once again, Dr La Pinta came to the rescue, concealing the seriousness of Cernan's injury:

"Geno we've got a serious injury here, but I'm not officially grounding you because I think we can lick it. You work with me, take it slow for a few days, and I'll get you ready on time. Far as anyone else is concerned, I'll tell 'em it's no big deal."

Cernan's conditions were still causing him problems as he suited up for the launch of Apollo 17:

"Chuck La Pinta and I grinned at each other as I squeezed my aching butt and sore leg into my space suit. When asked how I felt, I lied a little and he knew it."

...and even during his final EVA on the lunar surface, as Cernan reports:

"The stretched tendon in my leg hurt with every step I took."

Harrison Schmitt, Apollo 17

According to the official account, geologist Dr Harrison 'Jack' Schmitt was the last man to step onto the Moon's surface and the penultimate human being to leave it. As you consider his career as an astronaut, and subsequently (and briefly!) as a United States Senator, you may possibly ask yourself the question 'Aren't any of these people normal?'

Originally selected as a Scientist-Astronaut for the Apollo 18 mission, Schmitt had overseen the geological training of his fellow Moonwalkers. The cancellation of the final three Apollo missions had left Schmitt without a ride to the Moon, but pressure from fellow-geologists led to him replacing Joe Engle as LM Pilot.

This decision was apparently vindicated when Schmitt selected for collection 741 individual samples of lunar soil and rock, with a total mass of 111 kg: among these was a 3 metre drill core. This material has, we are told, produced invaluable data about the age of the Moon and the formation of its craters and maria basins. (Seas!)

But here's an interesting experiment for you to try! Put on half a dozen pairs of trousers, four or five sweaters and three pairs of thick gardening gloves. To these, add a scuba mask. Then see how long it takes you to place 741 pieces of rock (on average the size of a small potato) into ziplock bags: these then need to be packed and sealed into two large boxes.

That's an approximation of what Cernan & Schmitt allegedly accomplished! According to NASA:

The Apollo Lunar Sample Return Container (ALSRC) was an aluminum box with a triple seal manufactured by the Nuclear Division of Union Carbide. (Two of these) were used on each Apollo lunar landing mission to preserve a lunar-like vacuum around the samples and protect them from the shock environment of the return flight to earth. An aluminum mesh liner helped absorb impacts. Prior to flight, each box was loaded with sample container bags and other sample containment devices. The "rock box" was then closed under vacuum so that it would not contain pressure greater than the lunar ambient pressure. On the Moon, while samples were being loaded,

OUR FORBIDDEN MOON

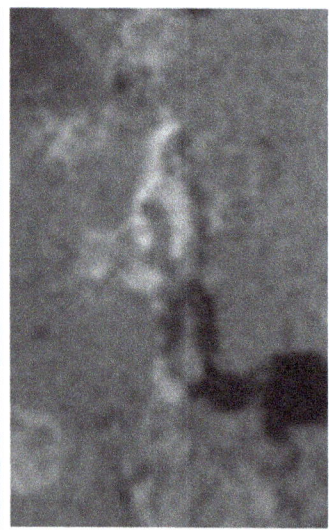

the seals were protected by a Teflon film and a cloth cover which were removed just prior to closing the box. A conveyor system was available, but the astronauts generally found it easier to carry the rock boxes up the lunar module's ladder.

The ALSRCs measured 20.3cm x 48.3cm x 29.8cm and had an unladen mass of 8.8kg. But it does strain one's credulity somewhat to imagine a Moonwalker wearing a clumsy suit and PLSS (Portable Life Support System) struggling up the LM ladder with a heavy and bulky metal container.

During each EVA, the Moonwalkers carried a PLSS on their back. As can be seen in the photo, this was a substantial bit of kit – and it needed to be: it was designed to help protect the astronauts against temperature swings, supply them with oxygen, remove carbon dioxide, control humidity and provide communications. Earlier, I mentioned a 'curious photograph' involving Dr Schmitt: this is it!

Look carefully at Schmitt's visor in the two images: the fourth picture is an enlarged version. A third person appears to be on the Moon with Schmitt and Cernan! What is more, he is obviously not wearing a PLSS! How is this possible? Well: only two solutions present themselves. Either the photograph was not taken on the Moon, or, if it was, then someone else was looking on!

At this point, now perhaps armed with enough relevant data, let's move forward from this scrutiny of the Apollo Moonwalkers to return to a question that was posed earlier: how many human beings – if any! – have actually walked on the Moon?

OUR FORBIDDEN MOON

CHAPTER 4:

THE 'C' WORD!

THERE is a word that is applied indiscriminately to any piece of popular debate, modern mythology or careful research that threatens the generally-held historical record. Make no mistake: there is a hidden agenda here. By use of the 'C word', the media, government and the industrial-military complex can sway public opinion and ridicule even the most assiduous researchers. Whether in respect to questioning anthropogenic global warming, the death of the Princess of Wales, Hitler's survival in 1945, the events of 911, the unexplained disappearance of an airliner or the divinity of Christ, this word is skilfully used to lump together dozens of completely unrelated, misreported or misinterpreted events.

It may interest the reader to learn that the term *'conspiracy theorist'* was coined and first used by the CIA in 1963 to undermine the credibility of anyone who suggested an alternative to the 'lone nut' explanation for the Kennedy assassination!

Any critical consideration of the Apollo landings or the UFO phenomenon are almost always targeted in this way. (Notice how many TV 'documentaries' on these topics are presented by comedians, committed cynics or people with no scientific credibility at all: Danny Dyer, Shaun Ryder, Mark Williams and – worst of all – Julia Bradbury – come immediately to mind.)

OUR FORBIDDEN MOON

This is strange: we don't come across a similar strategy of **'distort – misrepresent – ridicule – dismiss'** in other, apparently less contentious areas of human experience, even where the evidence used to justify them is dubious to say the least. A fortune has been spent on the Large Hadron Collider: It has so far cost over £10 billion, despite there being no evidence that the Higg's Boson (the sub-atomic particle which it was built to detect) actually exists.

Mission	Crew	Launch date	Details
Apollo 1	Grissom White Chaffee	21st February 1967	Crew killed in capsule fire, necessitating substantial redesign
Apollo 7	Schirra Eisele Cunningham	11th October 1968	First flight of manned Apollo CM. Crew removed from space flight roster because of their 'indiscipline'.
Apollo 8	Borman Lovell Anders	21st December 1968	First flight into lunar orbit.
Apollo 9	McDivvitt Scott Schweickart	3rd March 1969	First flight of LM (In Earth orbit)
Apollo 10	Stafford Young Cernan	18th May 1969	Second flight to Moon: LM descends within 15.6km of surface

The run up to the Moon landings: the official record

The same is true of the vast arrays of wind turbines and solar panels which are considered by many to be at best ineffective, at worst nett *consumers* of energy and nett *producers* of carbon dioxide during their construction and deployment, given their shorter-than-anticipated life spans.

Consider the timeline of events leading up to the missions outlined above. Between the disastrous Apollo 1 fire that necessitated the redesign of dozens of systems and engineering features and the alleged first successful landing of Apollo 11, a mere two and a half years elapsed.

Just twenty two months of R&D were required to take the Apollo Command and Service Modules from disaster to a triumphant orbit around the Moon: under thirty months following the near-cancellation of the Moon program after the disaster aboard Apollo 1, Young and Cernan swooped down to just over 8 miles from a touchdown on the Moon!

Does this seem almost too good to be true?

In my opinion the answer has to be an unqualified yes.

With just three unmanned system tests of the Saturn launch rocket and Apollo spacecraft (the last of which was very far from successful) before the first manned launch, this time frame stretches credibility to the limit.

A careful consideration of all the evidence seems inevitably to lead to the belief that the first attempted landing on the Moon could not have occurred before that of Apollo 15!

To sum up the suggestive evidence for this:

- The time frame for a capsule/systems rebuild and a complete revision of mission protocols and timings is completely unrealistic.
- The damage to US prestige of a withdrawal from the 'space race' with the Soviet Union and the potential political benefits of a successful fulfilment of Kennedy's pledge would not have been dismissed lightly.

- Thousands of jobs and billions of dollars of profit depended on NASA's continued participation in manned lunar exploration
- The TV and stills records of the Apollo 11, 12 and 14 missions do not bear scrutiny and contain innumerable anomalies.
- The crew selection of these missions and that of Apollo 13 are full of unexplained inconsistencies.
- The catastrophic explosion aboard the Apollo 13 spacecraft outbound to the Moon and the way the courageous crew managed to overcome every barrier to their safe return seems almost too good to be true.
- Even while the Apollo Moon missions were still taking place, many high profile commentators had begun to publically air their doubts about their reality.

Does the US government have a record of dissimulation to achieve what it considers worthwhile objectives? The answer would appear to be a resounding yes!

As a recent example, the Strategic Defence Initiative, the so-called 'Star Wars Program' of President Ronald Reagan, came, we are now told, desperately close to precipitating the world into global thermonuclear war. However, it ultimately achieved its goal of bringing down the Soviet Union by bankrupting it and convincing its leaders that they had no hope of matching the technological achievements of the United States. It subsequently transpired that even a feasibility study into SDI would have taken at least ten years with little hope of a workable solution!

Another, more recent example is the fabrication of evidence for the existence of Iraqi 'weapons of mass destruction' as a rationale for the first and second Gulf Wars.

It is at least possible that Apollo could have set a precedent for this strategy: but was there something else involved in the need to delay the Moon landings or even cancel the whole program?

CHAPTER 5:

OUR FORBIDDEN MOON

THERE is ample evidence that all is not as it purports to be in the official record of the Apollo Moon landings: the behaviour of the crew members before, during and since their missions, the anomalies associated with the lunar surface samples, the many contradictions in the testimonies of astronauts, mission controllers, scientists and photographic experts.... These all seem to suggest that the entire program may have been an extremely well-executed charade, designed to fulfil President Kennedy's promise to the American people and provide them with the national pride that such an achievement could have been expected to engender.

As we have seen, there is plenty of suggestive evidence that many major players in the US space program and in the world of military aviation had a firm belief in the existence of EBEs (extraterrestrial biological entities). Furthermore, the testimonies of many high-ranking officers – and even politicians – both then and in the present day – appear to confirm that some form of dialogue had started in the 1940s between one or more extraterrestrial races and an elite group of industrialists and military and intelligence officers on Earth.

We may never know the exact details of this alien liaison, or who was 'in the know', but there are plenty of credible books and websites that suggest

OUR FORBIDDEN MOON

it might have been a very small group of influential individuals. (Often referred to as 'MJ-12' or 'Majestic 12'.)

A number of investigators have suggested that the Apollo astronauts were not the first lunar explorers: one of the earliest was the author George Leonard, whose widely-ridiculed findings were presented in his book *"Somebody Else Is On The Moon"*, first published in 1976. It must be admitted that *in the paperback version*, the photographic evidence is less than convincing: the reader is invited to consider small, grainy images and interpret them as huge artificial structures.

However, online examination of some of the images in higher definition do seem to reveal apparently artificial structures, including domes, walled enclosures and obelisks.

It is worth reflecting that as early as 1953, John O'Neill, science editor for the *New York Herald Tribune*, announced his discovery of an enormous bridge on the edge of the Mare Crisium, in the top-right quarter of the Moon's disc. British astronomers HP Wilkins and Patrick Moore claimed to have viewed the object, Dr Wilkins describing the structure in a BBC radio interview: when asked if he could have been mistaken, Wilkins replied:

"Oh, no, there's no mistake at all. It's been confirmed by other observers. It looks artificial."

When asked to clarify "artificial," he replied,

"Well, it looks almost like an engineering job."

Perhaps unsurprisingly, these observations were quickly ridiculed and there is little doubt that the reputations of Wilkins and Moore were to suffer as a result. Whatever it may or may not have been, the bridge was mentioned by Major Donald E. Keyhoe in in his 1955 book, *The Flying Saucer Conspiracy*.

As an interesting aside, Sir Patrick Moore almost certainly once co-wrote a book (under the *nom de plume* Cedric Allingham) in which he claimed to have met a man from Mars. Perhaps this harmless hoax was Sir Patrick's response to his treatment by some of his peers during the Moon Bridge episode. I once asked him if he would like to confirm his involvement, mentioning the fact that the 12.5" reflecting telescope illustrated in the book was obviously his well-known instrument: he just smiled!

A more wide-ranging and influential book on more or less the same topic as Leonard's is **'Dark Mission – the secret history of NASA'** by Richard Hoagland. Chances are that anyone reading the present work will already be familiar with Hoagland's, so suffice it say, that using NASA photographs, he postulates that the Moon was formerly occupied by a technologically superior race who constructed bases within vast transparent domes. Certainly, many of the book's high quality illustrations seem to show the shattered remains of these ancient structures.

OUR FORBIDDEN MOON

Again, Hoagland's work (while enjoying wide popular interest) has predictably attracted casual dismissal, presumably from those who believe that our governments never keep anything secret from us!

In the introduction to his book, Hoagland includes an incredible (yet underplayed) quote from a 1959 study by the Brookings Institution, officially titled "Proposed Studies on the Implications of Peaceful Space Activities for Human Affairs."

"While face-to-face meetings with [extraterrestrial life] will not occur within the next 20 years (unless its technology is more advanced than ours, [allowing] it to visit Earth), artefacts left at some point in time by these life forms might possibly be discovered through [NASA's] space activities on the Moon, Mars, or Venus."

Ignoring the over-optimistic possibility of *anything* surviving long enough on the surface of Venus to carry out any form of exploration, this is a pretty interesting paragraph. As Hoagland comments:

"Brookings officially affirmed NASA's expectations that the Agency would fly to nearby planets in the solar system, and would thus be physically capable, for the first time, of confronting "extraterrestrials" right in their backyard"

As we have seen earlier, there appears to be suggestive evidence that this expectation was the result of contacts- accidental or planned – between pilots and astronauts and extraterrestrial spacecraft. And, if we are to believe the accounts of some sources within the former Soviet Union, this may even have included encounters with their crews:

Col. Marina Popovich was the widow of Cosmonaut and UFO researcher Pavel Popovich. She flew over 100 types of aircraft and has been called the 'Chuck Yeager of Russia'. She held ninety international flight records, and has a Ph.D. in engineering sciences.

In e-mails to me before her death in 2017 and during public debates, she stated that:

- Russian satellites have taken many photographs of flying saucers.
- Russian scientists have concluded that flying saucers have been around for as long as our planet.
- She has seen photographs of alien / human hybrid children.

Additionally, there have been persistent rumours of a very close encounter between 'angel-like' entities and the crew of Soviet space station Salyut 7. (Cosmonauts Svetlana Savitskaya, Igor Volk, Leonid Kizim, Oleg Atkov, Vladimir Solovyov, and Vladimir Jannibekov.)

Is it not within the realms of possibility that, almost as soon as mankind ventured into space in 1961, extraterrestrial civilizations that had been using our Moon as a base of operations began monitoring our activities? Perhaps the initial low Earth orbit missions of Vostok, Mercury, Voskhod and Gemini were not perceived as a problem by their leaders or our own clandestine liaison groups. But Kennedy's bold commitment to a Man on the Moon by 1970 may have been a step too far towards a general disclosure that someone else has a presence on our Moon.

Was Kennedy aware of this? And was he involved in the postulated Apollo deception? I think that is unlikely. The best way to keep something secret is on a 'need to know' basis: since Presidents and Prime Ministers tend only to occupy their office for one or two short terms, it seems unlikely that they would be 'in the loop'. It is a commonly held belief within the 'UFO fraternity' that the last US President in whom the security agencies confided was Harry S Truman or possibly (given his high military rank) Dwight D Eisenhower. Of course, there may be a significance in Ronald Reagan's well-known and somewhat cryptic remark in an address to the UN:

"I occasionally think about how quickly our differences worldwide would vanish, if we were facing an alien threat from outside this world. And yet, I ask you, is not an alien force already among us?"

President Reagan is alleged to have had two personal UFO encounters, so perhaps his comments were personal musings, rather than the result of a formal briefing by the US intelligence services.

Nothing in the actions or public speeches of later Presidents suggests a detailed knowledge of the UFO phenomenon, nor a desire to push for full disclosure: despite many promises to reveal historical UFO archives and despite the Freedom of Information Act, what has actually been released, both in the US and the UK, is a carefully censored and bowdlerized précis.

Despite the apparent support for the space program of Bill Clinton and

OUR FORBIDDEN MOON

George W Bush, successive presidents have overseen the dismantling of NASA's ability to send manned craft into anything other than low orbit: and since Atlantis made her final flight in July 2011, the US has had to pay Russia for crew space aboard one of its aging Soyuz spacecraft. Does it not seem strange that America built and paid for most of the International Space Station, but since 2011 has had no way to travel to it, other than hitching a ride with its one-time Cold War enemy? What happens if Russia stops co-operating before NASA's own space program (or any of the private enterprise systems) are ready?

Given the national pride that resulted from NASA's achievements during its 'golden years' from 1961 to 1972, why has the United States tossed aside its pre-eminence in manned spaceflight?

There are a number of frequently offered explanations...

Finance

The most widely accepted reason for the USA's withdrawal from manned exploration of the Moon and inner planets is the high cost. With the decline of American industry, competition for global market share from China and India and the rise of Russia as a capitalist power, even the cost of replacing the aging Shuttle Orbiter fleet was deemed a luxury the country couldn't afford. But is this really credible? The cost of the entire Apollo Program including R&D of the Saturn 1 and V launch vehicles, the modular Apollo spacecraft and the Skylab / ASTP missions was reported to Congress to have been $23 billion. This might seem a lot, but the US has spent nearly a *thousand* times that amount prosecuting the so-called 'War On Terror'. To put it another way, if the US had decided not to take part in three largely unpopular actions in Iraq and Afghanistan, they could have gone to the Moon *six thousand times!* (Or, possibly, have built settlements there or on Mars.)

Additionally, it is often forgotten that grand projects like Apollo generate huge numbers of jobs. These lay not just in the aerospace industry, but peripherally in construction, technology, transport and many other areas, and resulted in the development of a myriad of innovations in bio-medical science, IT, materials technology etc. In fact, the Apollo Program - whether it actually took twelve men to the Moon or not - brought about a substantial rise in general standards of living in many regions within the USA. So money wasn't the problem!

Political will

It is evident that the US population, like that of many western nations, has undergone a significant change in personal belief systems and aspirations. In the 1950s, America had moved from isolationism to a self-appointed role as guardian of the free world. A US military presence was established in many European countries to defend NATO against the real or imagined threat of the Warsaw Pact: over twenty USAF airbases in the UK alone. American culture (in the shape of rock & roll, Coca Cola, burger bars, 'movies' and TV programmes) and American morality replaced that of her allies in Europe and the Far East. But increased personal wealth and freedom often come at a cost. At some point in the late fifties, the youth of America evolved their own sub-culture that began openly to question traditional values. By the time of the Apollo Program and its running-mate, the Vietnam War, young people had discovered their voice: they quickly rejected the notion that the 'Government Knows Best'. In this era of political assassinations, civil rights marches and protest songs, the idea of spending $23 billion dollars on what had always been promoted as essentially a prop to national pride suddenly didn't seem such a good deal.

Barry McGuire spoke for American kids in his song 'The Eve of Destruction':

Think of all the hate there is in Red China
Then take a look around to Selma, Alabama
You may leave here for four days in space

But when you return it's the same old place

Add to this the subtle redefining of the President's role from the man where the buck stopped to that of a virtual figurehead, notionally head of the armed forces and government but with limited personal action, whose policies are dictated to him by the industrial-military complex that *actually* makes the decisions.

At the time of writing, President Donald Trump has committed the US to a Moon landing in 2024. (This seems a little optimistic, but nevertheless shows that the current thinking is that a return to the Moon is both desirable and achievable. (Interestingly, the proposed landing site is near the lunar south pole: nowhere near the alleged Apollo sites!)

So if the problem isn't money or political will, what is it?

Extraterrestrial intervention

There can be little doubt that the factors outlined above had *some* influence on the direction of manned spaceflight in the US. But lack of popular support for a project or for its funding has never deflected any government from its purpose: there were very few supporters for any of the recent military actions in the 'War on Terror' and certainly they have had a dramatic impact on the economies of the US and UK.

It is worth reflecting on the fact that the Shuttle 'Space Transport System' was originally promoted to the American public as a way of making spaceflight as cheap and as routine as jet travel. That this was far from the case was demonstrated by the Challenger and Columbia disasters, which served to remind us all that space is a hostile environment: sitting on top of thousands of litres of highly explosive propellants is never going to be safe or 'routine'. By the final mission of the STS it seemed to most people that our collective vision of the future of spaceflight, fostered by films like '2001: A Space Odyssey ' and 'Star Wars' was further out of reach than it had been in

1972. So what went wrong? Did we somehow collectively lose the 'outward urge'? The boom in astronomical society memberships, new films and TV programs and telescope sales would suggest not. Do we lack the technology to travel to the Moon? The success of the many robotic probes to the Moon, Mars, comets, asteroids and the outer planets amply demonstrates that modern technology is vastly superior to that available in 1969.

To me, and to a growing number of veteran investigators, only one explanation seems plausible: **someone** slammed the gates to all but low Earth orbit.

One-time Canadian Minister of National Defence Paul Hellyer has had an interest in the UFO phenomenon for many years. Presumably, throughout a long political career, (Hellyer is currently the longest serving member of the Privy Council) he has used his position to accumulate data that would be inaccessible to most investigators. He has stated in various interviews and public meetings that:

"At least four species of alien have been visiting Earth for thousands of years. These species may have different agendas: not all are friendly towards mankind. There are extraterrestrials living on Earth at this present time: at least two of them are working with the United States government"

Hellyer has suggested that some of these aliens may see it as their mission to protect us from other, less friendly species.

What are we to make of this? We cannot continually disregard the high-credibility testimonies of public servants, military personnel, pilots and police officers purely on the basis that it doesn't fit in with our preconceptions or ingrained belief systems. People like Paul Hellyer, Col. Charles Halt and Col. Robert Salas have risked much by speaking out: they have all previously been trusted by us in their professional capacities (in Halt and Salas' cases as guardians of large inventories of nuclear weapons) so it's a little illogical not to do so now.

OUR FORBIDDEN MOON

Col. Charles Halt

The RH Paul Hellyer

Capt. Robert Salas

Col. Philip Corso

OUR FORBIDDEN MOON

Let us, for now, take Hellyer's testimony as being constructed around a central core of truth:

The human race has been in contact with alien beings for many years: some of them seem to provide us with the knowledge and technology required to protect us against other inimical species. It would seem possible that these friendly EBEs informed us in the past – perhaps around the time of the Roswell incident – that mankind faced clear and enduring danger from at least two other species.

As American pilots flew faster and higher and the first groups of Cosmonauts and Astronauts were selected, perhaps people began to reflect for the first time that mankind could soon be coming into contact with these – and perhaps other – alien races.

Although undoubtedly a somewhat controversial figure, Col. Philip Corso has given his version (based on his proven service within the military and intelligence communities) of the genuine concern that was voiced as early as the 1960s about alien activities endangering US space missions. Corso's book 'The Day After Roswell' reads like a work of fiction, but undoubtedly contains details that suggest the author really was privy to sensitive and restricted information. His contention is that the peoples of the Earth have been involved in a full-on conflict with at least one alien race for decades, before finally triumphing through the use of beam weapon technology given to us by the friendly extraterrestrials mentioned earlier.

This apparently incredible idea does have the merit of explaining many aspects of the UFO phenomenon. If it *is* the case that hostile (or at least inimical) alien races have for decades been operating from a base on the far side of the Moon, then the major objections about how small 'scout ship' UFOs could ever reach the Earth from distant star systems is irrelevant: rather than light years, they would only have to travel a quarter of a million miles. And if these bases are operated by more than one race, it might explain why UFOs seem to come in a wide range of shapes and sizes.

Many sceptics point to the apparent randomness of UFO / EBE activity: the whole package of abductions / animal mutilations / crop circles does seem too bizarre for them to be aspects of a single phenomenon. But of course, we have absolutely no idea what 'normal' means in relation to organisms that have evolved on distant worlds with different ecosystems millennia before the human race ever appeared on Earth. Perhaps the 'unfriendly' EBEs view us in the way we view lab rats or beagles: perhaps (even worse!) they see us as a protein source! **We're** not exactly considerate to the thousands of living entities with whom we share our planet: the rate of extinction we have caused is currently running at over 25,000 species a year!

At public talks about the UFO phenomenon, one of the most frequently-made comments is:

"Why travel all the way here from, say, Zeta Reticuli just to collect a bucket of water, excise a cow's anus or conduct an endoscopy on a hillbilly? Why not land on the lawn of the White House?"

The assumption being made here is, of course, that our putative EBE visitors *want* to involve themselves in an open dialogue with our leaders. But all the evidence suggests that, for thousands of years, they have purposely kept their activities hidden. The reason for this could be quite straightforward: the hostile EBEs gain nothing by openly revealing their interest in us, while the friendly species – and those humans who are 'in the know' – probably anticipate dramatic social and political upheavals.

But perhaps all this is about to change: perhaps the ready accessibility to information provided by the World Wide Web has seriously eroded the possibility of keeping UFOs a secret. Those who have been attempting to do so may now have no choice but to gradually drip-feed the truth to us. It certainly does seem as if Hollywood and the TV companies have a policy of promoting a 'good aliens / bad aliens' vision, while we are subjected to

OUR FORBIDDEN MOON

subliminal images of flying saucers in the most unlikely places. (Even in the opening credits of the BBC quiz game 'Pointless'!) Perhaps when the public seems suitably receptive we can, at last, anticipate full disclosure...

The many inconsistencies in the official accounts of the Apollo landings and the apparent failure of our spacecraft to leave low Earth orbit could

Positive alien themes	Negative alien themes
'Batteries Not Included'	'Species'
'ET'	'War of the Worlds'
'Close Encounters'	'Cloverfield'
'Dave'	'Signs'
'Paul'	'Independence Day'

both be explained if it were the case that we have – for our own good – been placed in quarantine on our home planet.

So will mankind ever visit or colonise the Moon? I once asked an Apollo astronaut this question (Of course, I used the verb 'return'!) His answer was not optimistic. He responded: "How old are you, Buddy?" I told him I was 60. He added: "Well *you* ain't going to live long enough to see it!" At the time, President Obama had decided to pull the plug on the Ares / Constellation program. Was it just this that had made the astronaut so pessimistic, or did he know something we don't?

OUR FORBIDDEN MOON

APPENDIX 1

TOO GOOD TO BE TRUE? APOLLO 13

IN the traumatic era of post-Cuba crisis, shocking assassinations of popular political figures and disastrous involvement in South-East Asia, the American people seemingly grew bored with the whole enterprise of Moon travel almost as soon as the Apollo 11 ticker-tape had been swept up. It is absolutely true that, soon after TLI, the live feed from Apollo 13 was dropped by major networks in favour of the Doris Day TV show! Then came the incident aboard the spacecraft's Service Module: while a 'cryo-stir' was being remotely carried out in a liquid oxygen tank, a spark from a damaged electrical cable caused a fire which heated the tank, resulting in a devastating explosion.

Overnight, Apollo became news again: all around the world people held their breath as they followed the unfolding drama of the crippled spacecraft's predicament. Against all the odds the crew overcame electrical undervoltages, a potentially fatal carbon dioxide build-up, loss of much of their oxygen and water reserves and the navigational shortcomings of the Command Module's flight computer.

As we watched and listened in real time, Apollo 13 swung around the Moon, returned to Earth and completed a copy-book splashdown just four miles from the recovery ship *USS Iwo Jima*. The potential loss of the spacecraft

OUR FORBIDDEN MOON

and its crew was averted, we are told, by the resourcefulness and courage of mission controllers, flight engineers, the three astronauts and the crew member they left behind, Ken Mattingly. (It was feared he might have been exposed to measles and, despite his receiving only two days orientation for this specific mission, John 'Jack' Swigert replaced him just three days before launch!)

Honestly, ask yourself: if the Apollo 13 mission had never taken place and Ron Howard's famous film had been made as a piece of pure entertainment, wouldn't most of us have considered the events portrayed as being just too far-fetched? We are told that every Apollo mission was rated with only a 50% probability of a safe conclusion: how much less likely then, that such a severely crippled spacecraft could function as flawlessly as we are asked to believe?

In our consideration of the credibility of the Apollo 13 legend, there is an apparently minor feature of the mission that is worth examination: the strange case of the LiOH canisters.

Human beings – like all aerobic respirers, including plants – produce the waste products carbon dioxide and water. If the CO2 concentration in the air we breathe in reaches 3% (30,000 ppm) we begin to experience nausea and confusion: levels above 5% will ultimately be fatal.

In the sealed environment of a spacecraft, the CO2 must be removed by circulating the air through filters containing reagents such as lithium hydroxide: this binds the gas as a carbonate. When the filter becomes saturated, it can be changed for a new one. On the Apollo 13 mission the astronauts were forced to complete much of the return journey to Earth aboard the LM and although there was sufficient oxygen for the LM crew and CM pilot, 'Aquarius' did not, apparently, have sufficient CO2 scrubbing capacity for all three. The Command Module 'Odyssey' had plenty of spare LiOH canisters, but these, were square and couldn't be inserted into the circular housing on board the Lunar Module. Hmmmm!

Apollo 13

Apollo 15

Apollo 17

It is, of course, the case that the Command Module and Lunar Module were built by two different contractors: North American Aviation and Grumman respectively. Are we really to believe that they never considered using the same filter elements for both spacecraft? That just doesn't make sense! Firstly, the many mission simulations carried out during R&D must have thrown up the possibility that one module might have needed replenishment from the other. Secondly, strategic logistical planning demands using a single contractor for each type of consumable. It's the only way to guarantee uniformity and quality. (Many of you may have experienced the results of similarly poor planning when a 'pattern' car spare doesn't actually fit your model!

So years of planning and billions of dollars of research, simulation and development failed to recognise this crucial design flaw

As Americans say: *"That dog don't hunt!"*

What is possibly less well-known about the Apollo 13 mission is that the Saturn V launch rocket suffered a potentially disastrous second stage engine cut off during the climb up to orbit. Soviet Cosmonaut Alexei Leonov once remarked to me that he always felt that the Soviet Soyuz launch vehicle was inherently much safer: the failure of one or two of its twenty clustered rocket motors would not have resulted in a catastrophic asymmetrical thrust as the failure of one of the Saturn rocket's four outer motors. With the same incredible good fortune that seems to typify the Apollo 13 mission, the motor that failed was the central one of the S-11 stage!

A last thing for the reader to consider:

When the Command Module undocked from the Service Module, the crew took their first look at the 'tremendous damage' it had suffered in the explosion and fire that had ripped it apart and blown off the 'entire Plate 4 panel'. The photograph they took of the devastation has been widely published, reinforcing our astonishment at the crew's survival. But hang on! Look at the photographs of the Service Modules taken on two other Apollo missions. Notice anything? Compared to the other two, the Apollo 13 Service Module doesn't seem significantly damaged, does it?

OUR FORBIDDEN MOON

APPENDIX 2

THE STRANGE HISTORY OF THE APOLLO MOONROCKS

TO many people, one of the greatest achievements of the Apollo Program was the collection and return to Earth of 380kg of rocks and soil. However, these samples may not necessarily represent concrete proof that man has visited the Moon!

The Apollo lunar material is stored in an atmosphere of nitrogen at the Lunar Sample Laboratory Facility at the Johnson Space Center, Houston, Texas. A reserve collection is kept at White Sands, New Mexico.

From time to time small fragments of rock are allowed out for testing at other facilities: this is carried out under the most stringent security: and no wonder! When a few tiny samples were stolen from Houston in 2002 they were valued by NASA (for the court hearing after their recovery) at $1,000,000 for 285g Just suppose for a minute that you are a research planetary geologist or mineralogist. You ask NASA for access to a small sample to work on. After much negotiation and legal discussion, a pair of security guards arrives at your pre-scrutinised facility in an armoured vehicle. The material (probably a few milligrams) is delivered to you in a portable safe: you are required to sign a receipt that carries a description of the material and states its exact mass.

OUR FORBIDDEN MOON

Under these circumstances, would it ever cross your mind during your examination that you were not working with the genuine article, brought back from the Moon by Apollo astronauts? Having performed your tests, you may well have found that your sample is chemically not too dissimilar to the anorthosites or basalts found on Earth. But that's not surprising, is it? Hasn't NASA proved that the Earth and Moon system was formed by a massive collision billions of years ago that left both with pretty much the same crustal rock chemistry?

To put it plainly: we all believe that these 380kg of rocks originated on the Moon because the very organisation having a vested interest in fostering that belief ***told us so!***

Perhaps surprisingly, the vast majority of the Apollo samples – well over 300kg – have never been examined by independent researchers, being 'archived for posterity' at the LSLF in Houston. (Interestingly, since the Apollo Program finished, over 100 meteorites, with a total mass of around 250kg, have been identified as being lunar in origin: many of these are also stored at the LSLF!)

To date, no lunaites have actually been seen falling from the sky, and a perceptive reader may wonder how their origin is known with near-certainty. These objects are undoubtedly meteoritic, showing the characteristic signs of high speed ablation: regmaglypts (depressions resembling thumb prints in wet clay) a dark fusion crust and orientation. They are classified as achondrites, a type of meteorite which originated on a fully-differentiated planetary body and which are much younger than the more abundant chondrites. Additionally, the comparative amounts of several isotopes found in lunaites makes it certain that if they did not come the Moon, they can only have originated on Earth!

At the time of the alleged Moon landings, only three mineral samples brought back by the Apollo Moonwalkers were found to be unknown on

OUR FORBIDDEN MOON

Earth: armalcolite, pyroxferroite and tranquillityite. Curiously, and perhaps significantly, all three have since been discovered in terrestrial rocks!

Surely there is something very suggestive about the fact that the 'Goodwill Moonrock' given to former Dutch Prime Minister Willem Drees during a tour by the three Apollo 11 astronauts in 1969 has been identified as a piece of fossil wood...

Finally – and most intriguingly – a rock 'brought back from the Moon' by the Apollo 14 astronauts was found (in January 2019) to be terrestrial in origin! The explanation for this inconvenient discovery (by Jeremy Bellucci and Alexander Nemchin at the Swedish Museum of Natural History and Curtin University in Australia) is that the rock was blasted from the Earth millions of years ago, arriving on the Moon as a meteorite.

But wait a minute! Are we supposed to believe that among the mere 42kg of rocks and soil collected by the Apollo 14 mission, one was a *meteorite from Earth?*

Of course, most of the Moon's craters are meteoric or cometary in origin, but the vast majority of these will have been made by asteroidal or other debris. Terrestrial meteorites do undoubtedly exist – some brachinites have the same relative oxygen isotope composition as Earth rocks - but such meteorites are incredibly rare even on Earth: much rarer than lunar meteorites. Of course, applying Occam's famous razor, there is *another* possibility for the origin of this inconvenient piece of rock!

Possibly the strangest thing about the Apollo moon rocks, given the rigour with which NASA guards them, is the fact that quite a few have gone missing! 5kgs of this precious material were allocated as goodwill donations to a variety of recipients: museums and other similar institutions, world leaders and each of the 50 American states. Astonishingly, at the time of writing the whereabouts of 180 of the 270 samples is not known!

APPENDIX 3

THE DEVIL IS IN THE DETAIL: DUMMIES, BUGGIES AND CGI

ON one of the occasions when I met Capt. Alan Bean, the Apollo 12 Moonwalker, he was kind enough to examine some of my space artwork and give me some helpful advice about how to add authenticity to my efforts. After a general chat about light and shadow, he moved on to a discussion about the difficulties he experienced in getting the reflections right on the helmets of the astronaut figures in his paintings. He confided in me that he'd been:

'...given a tip by the photography guys I knew from the program. They told me to use little models of astronauts, with their heads replaced by steel ball-bearings: this I did, placing them into a suitable background and lighting this scene up with a spotlight. That way I found I could adjust the light and get things just right.'

Some time later I realised what an interesting statement this was. Who were these 'photography guys' and why had they developed this strategy for adjusting the lighting of a lunar landscape?

Since the first edition of this book was published, I've looked even more closely into the images and videos that were allegedly taken during the six

OUR FORBIDDEN MOON

Plate 19: The author discussing his art with Capt. Bean

Moon landings, and have come to believe that Capt. Bean – consciously or unconsciously – might have been intimating that some of them may not show real astronauts, lunar rovers and LMs at all. Is it possible that at least some of the Apollo images are actually of scale models and mannikins?

For fifty or more years people have questioned the authenticity of the Apollo photography, generally basing their arguments around the angles

OUR FORBIDDEN MOON

of shadows on the lunar surface and apparent anomalies with the cross-hair graticules on some of the pictures.

I personally feel that *some* of the 'shadow evidence' is overstated: it is entirely possible to replicate many of the images with diverging shadows (supposedly the result of the use of multiple light sources) on Earth, with the Sun as the sole illumination. I think the direction of the shadows owes much to the angle of the landscape and the effects of perspective. In similar fashion, I have managed to reproduce some of the supposed cross-hair anomalies in my back garden by playing around with focus, ISO, exposure and f-stop settings. (See Plate 20)

There are other problems, however, that seem impossible to resolve.

In a large number of images in the NASA Apollo catalogue, tiny astronaut figures are used to suggest distance and scale. With modern image-handling software, it's possible to zoom in on these: in a surprising number of cases a set of three or four images palpably show exactly the same figure, apparently frozen in some task-related action pose. My contention is that small mannikins – perhaps less than a metre tall – were used on carefully-built sets to give the impression of an astronaut working hundreds of metres from the camera. This same mechanism is often used in museum dioramas: my local Norwich Castle has several that illustrate Broadland and Breckland landscapes.

One common criticism of the Moon photos is that shadows are not parallel: Here we see that the direction of shadows can depend on topography and perspective.

OUR FORBIDDEN MOON

Plate 20: Shadow and graticule effects resolved? Note how the graticule lines are apparently behind the objects in the first three images (taken on the Moon). The fourth image shows an identical effect, produced by over-exposure of a bright subject.

If you examine the Apollo 14 image below, there is something of the 'too good to be true' about it: the astronaut and LM are seen in the distance, suggesting that the photographer (Edgar Mitchell) is **at least** a hundred metres away. Look closely: there is an obvious delineation between the figure of Shepard, the LM and the mountains and foothills behind. To me, this image is one of many that seem to have been shot in a carefully lit indoor set. The backdrop of hills and dark, starless sky is actually a set-dressing mounted on the back wall, while the astronaut figure and LM are models, placed to create the impression of distance. Notice the sharp footprint in

Plate 21: So near, yet so far away!

the left foreground, with the suggestion of a trail leading back towards the LM: again, this gives the illusion that Mitchell is standing a few hundred metres from the Lunar Module, watching his Commander walking away into the distance. Variants of this scene appear in the photographic records of virtually every mission.

Further evidence of the use of scale models and mannikins comes from still and video imagery of the Lunar Roving Vehicle (LRV or Rover) employed by the final three purported lunar landing missions, Apollos 15, 16 & 17. Numerous photos, as we have seen, show the Rover motionless among dozens of footprints, but with **absolutely no tyre tracks!** This in itself is, to say the least, hard to explain: but there is more!

Recent television documentaries have used footage of astronauts training with the Rover in Arizona and at Cape Canaveral. What becomes immediately apparent is that two or three people were required to help the astronauts stand up and climb from the Rover: from a semi-supine position, with their legs stretched out in front and with the heavy PLSS (Personal Life Support System) strapped on their backs the Apollo astronauts seemingly found it impossible to shift their centres of gravity over their feet and stand up without assistance. It comes as no surprise, therefore, to note that **not a single video** allegedly taken on the Moon shows an astronaut climbing from his seat on the Lunar Rover.

If you make the effort to seek out NASA video sequences online of EVAs using the Rover, you will be struck, as I was, by how high the plumes of dust are thrown up behind the vehicle as it travels across the Moon's surface. This could *not* be replicated by a full-sized Rover in a studio on Earth. However, a quarter-sized scale model generates exactly the right effect. What's more, if you slow the majority of these Rover videos down, you'll notice the curious immobility of the astronauts: they sit upright, barely moving their heads or arms at all. I would suggest that a possible reason might be that we are looking at lifelike mannikins. I can only conclude from these and other pieces of evidence that the still and video record of the Apollo lunar landings are in fact a combination of studio shots using both full- and reduced-sized replicas of astronauts and their hardware and of CGI (computer generated imagery).

Most of the Apollo image catalogue is not available for commercial reproduction without a license – and I doubt that one would be forthcoming for a work such as this! But even half an hour's searching online will allow you to check the accuracy of my references: if you then experiment using software such as Paintshop or Irfanview, I have absolutely no doubt that you will be amazed at what you discover. Evidence of CGI, retouching and model-use is everywhere!

OUR FORBIDDEN MOON

APPENDIX 4

BEGINNINGS

I AM often asked during my talks to Astronomical Societies whether I really believe in the reality of the UFO phenomenon. Long ago, I made the decision to 'shame the devil and tell the truth' and always reply in the affirmative. This often results in a heated discussion, which I generally silence by giving accounts of my own experiences. It is astonishing how frequently this has encouraged members of the audience to add their own observations!

Here are some of my most interesting encounters, that began when I was just six years old!

1957! What a year! Two great comets visited the inner solar system and awoke many a young mind to an interest in Astronomy! And I was one of them! Ever since those long-distant days I have spent more time looking up to the stars than down into the gutter...

I was, at the time, in my second year at North Street Primary School in what was then the small quiet town of Hornchurch, Essex.

As the author L P Hartley remarked at the start of his novel, **'The Go-Between':**

'The past is a foreign country: they do things differently there...'

OUR FORBIDDEN MOON

In those days it was considered perfectly acceptable for a child to walk unaccompanied to school with a reasonable chance of a safe arrival! My mother had developed the charming tradition of walking much of the way with me, pausing at a baker's shop to buy a cake to keep me amused during my one-hour wait in the playground for the caretaker to arrive and unlock the school.

On this particular morning, I found myself (as usual) alone, eagerly anticipating the arrival of my playmates. I gazed upwards into the post-dawn skies: immediately I found my gaze drawn towards a most extraordinary object. Directly above, travelling slowly West to East was an intensely bright silver disc. Behind it trailed what I can only describe as a plume of fire-flecked grey smoke. I watched fascinated as the amazing object scintillated in the cold, early morning sunlight, for as well as its linear motion from horizon to horizon, the strange object also rocked like a slowly-falling leaf.

Eventually the silent visitor disappeared into the distance, leaving me perplexed and a little disturbed. My solitary reverie was broken by the arrival of Miss Church, the spinster Headmistress of the School. Naturally, I could not wait to tell her my tale. Somewhat disconcertingly, she smiled!

"Come to my office, child, and tell me more!"

she said. I dutifully followed. Even more bizarrely, she then invited me to sit upon her bony lap while I told my tale! After I'd finished, she unfolded a newspaper to reveal the cover photograph of what I now know to have been the comet Arend Roland. She spoke again:

"Astronomy has long been a passion of mine, child! How wonderful to find a kindred spirit in one so young!"

I did not have the heart to disabuse the elderly woman: as young as I was, I knew I had not been looking at a comet! Still, she was right: the events of that long-gone, day stayed with me my whole life. Astronomy became a passion, an element of my subsequent university studies, part of the reason I joined the Royal Navy as a pilot and, of course, the inspiration for a life-long study of the UFO phenomenon.

When I left the Navy, I was forced to look for something to keep me occupied until college started in the Autumn: I found myself working in a garage in the town of Shenfield, just outside of London. I had to leave the house in which I was living very early in the morning so that I might arrive in time for my shift at the pumps! I always rode to work on a 'bus: accordingly my day began at a bus-stop at a curiously named spot called 'Hanging Hill Lane' in the leafy suburb of Hutton. On this particular morning in 1970, I shared my vigil at the bus-stop with a group of perhaps fifteen women, all of whom were on their way to commence their shifts at the Selo factory in nearby Brentwood.

OUR FORBIDDEN MOON

It was well before dawn, yet the promise of sunrise was in the sky. I happened to glance towards the eastern horizon, when over the top of the bungalows that fringed this quiet residential avenue came a half-echelon of the most extraordinary craft.

Catching the rays of the still horizontal Sun, three huge circular vehicles scintillated in the dark pre-dawn skies. I would have to say they were at least twice the size of a Jumbo jet, and passed across the sky to the zenith in complete silence at an altitude of perhaps three thousand metres,: at this point they passed into the dark umbra of the Earth, so that their passage to the Western horizon could only be followed by the stars they eclipsed!

The middle aged women became hysterical when I pointed out the phenomenon to them!

One final, perhaps significant occurrence…..about five minutes after the strange visitors disappeared from view, a pair of jet fighter aircraft followed in their path:- English Electric Lightnings, I seem to recall. Were

OUR FORBIDDEN MOON

these interceptors chasing the craft? It certainly seemed so to the ladies, who cheered and clapped as if they were watching a western movie!

In the late 1970s.I was driving home from the beautiful city of Norwich to Great Yarmouth with my first wife, a teacher friend and his two young children. Our journey took us along a dark, lonely stretch of road that wound between the villages of Acle and Wroxham. The night was moonless and dark, yet, being early autumn, warm and somewhat humid. Suddenly the road ahead was illuminated by a blinding blue-white cone of light that was descending vertically from above! I slowed to a halt: already my ex-wife had become anxious and demanded that I drive on.

The light vanished as abruptly as it had appeared, but looking up, a black circular shadow could be discerned, travelling across the sky, eclipsing the stars as it did so....

Twice more the blinding cone of light lit up the fields to the south of the road: as this happened, a humming noise like a cheap child's top could be heard. My ex- wife had by now become nearly hysterical, so I threw the car into gear, and sped off in a spray of gravel. As I rounded the tree-girt bend at the end of the long straight where this astonishing event had occurred, a glance in the mirror provided a further view of the strange visitor.

Perhaps twenty years after these events occurred, my old friend (with whom I had lost contact after he had moved to Yorkshire) happened to come across my name on the internet and e-mailed me his version of events!

"Hi David, Having just read your name on a website, I was moved to contact you and remind you of the astonishing UFO experience we shared.

I do remember it a little differently. We were returning from Norwich after a day's work. You were driving and had your first wife in the back with my two oldest children. It was between four and five and just getting dark as we drove home. I was sitting next to you in the front. As we travelled down the very long straight section of road between Little Plumstead and Panxworth, we both noticed a bright, white, downward facing light over to our right. It was like the cone of a strong search light. Behind it were dimmer, yellow lights, arranged like port holes. It was coming towards us at an oblique angle, from the right as you were driving towards it. I remember jokingly pointing at it and whistling the five note sequence from 'Close Encounters' I think we thought it was an aircraft coming in to land at Norwich Airport. However as the distance closed between us, we came to realise just how big the scale of whatever it was we were looking at.

The white cone of light was well into the fields on the left of the road, while the yellow lights stretched way over the road into the fields on the right of the road.

We realised we were going to drive under it, it was moving very slowly from right to left, and seemed to be about 100 feet off the ground. At this point we all felt quite scared but utterly fascinated by what we were looking at. The road then bent sharp left down a short bank, then turned right before a climb out of the depression. It was tree lined: the children used to call it Dingly Dell. At the bottom of the bank was a field entrance, which you pulled into and stopped. You turned off the engine, and we opened the windows to look at the lights. They had continued into the field, and stopped, hovering over a circular copse of trees, just on the outskirts of Panxworth, between the road we were on and Salhouse Road. The thing that unsettled me was that it was totally silent! A seemingly massive craft was hovering with no engine noise, 100 feet off the ground, just skimming the trees. Now here is the thing that I will never understand: why didn't we go and investigate this phenomenon?

This moment was a godsend to enquiring minds, yet suddenly we all felt really unnerved, got back in the car, and fled from the scene. You dropped the children and me off in South Walsham, at the bottom of Flowerdew's Lane. We walked up to the cottage, got my ex wife outside, pointed across the valley, and you could still see the lights hovering over the trees!

I have no idea what it was we saw that evening, though I have tried to rationally analyze it. An aircraft that big would have had to move fairly quickly to keep flying, and would have made some engine noise. There was a dirigible kept at the airport, which could appear to hover, but was much smaller, and even that had a propeller: a helicopter is an incredibly noisy thing.

I have recently read about low frequency wave generators that can cause a feeling of unease and panic, which may, perhaps, account for our sudden change of mood."

OUR FORBIDDEN MOON

There is a sequel! Some years later my journey home from Gt.Yarmouth took me along some of these beautiful country lanes that, as described above, wind sinuously towards Norwich through small copses and fields of rape and sugar beet.

One afternoon in the late Spring I was reaching the end of my drive homeward when I slowed to allow an almost black pheasant to scramble across the road in front of my van. As I followed his progress into a field of lush grass, my attention was grabbed by a movement against the patchy clouds. Moving slowly over the fields towards a line of oak trees was a classic 'Flying Saucer', about ten to fifteen metres across, this circular, metallic object emitted no sounds or light as it moved over the woods at an altitude of perhaps thirty metres before disappearing from view! Having a 'shoot and click' camera with me, I had time to take a single photograph.

This encounter took place at the approach to 'Dingly Dell', the location described above!

APPENDIX 5

RENDLESHAM FOREST

A MAJOR passion of mine is wildlife watching: I have enjoyed looking at and photographing animals and plants for over fifty years and it was, in fact, through birdwatching that Linda and I got together.

I became aware of the Rendlesham and Tunstall Forests back in the mid-eighties: just before the famous 'non-hurricane' of 1987, these were fantastic places to find some really unusual birds such as Hawfinches and Firecrests. Linda and I first visited together in, I think, 1989 to look for a White-tailed Eagle.

On my first trip to the woods, I stopped to chat to a forest ranger, who asked if I had heard about the 'Goings-on of 1980' I hadn't, but he soon filled me in! I now realise most of his account was, to say the least, imaginative! Back in 1983 I don't believe any books about the RFI had been published: I certainly wasn't aware of them. But then, as one by one they were released, I began to grow interested in the events of Christmas, 1980 and have since visited the Forest many times, usually with Linda and long-time enthusiasts Jason Hughes and Paul Williams. We have had very many strange experiences that I cannot begin to understand: even Paul (with his healthy scepticism) has been impressed by some of the images and video anomalies we have collected.

Colonel Charles Halt and the author in Rendlesham Forest

OUR FORBIDDEN MOON

Over the years, my interest in the so-called Rendlesham Forest Incident has allowed me to meet most of the major personalities in this, the UK's most famous UFO case. These range from the ultra-professional and credible Deputy Base Commander, Col. Charles Halt, to the two Security Guards, Airman John Burroughs and Staff Sergeant Jim Penniston, who were the first to witness the strange events of December 1980. Other 'witnesses' have subsequently been revealed to be untrustworthy and even mendacious, but it is my firm opinion that this isolated forest on the edge of East Anglia genuinely was the location of an extra-terrestrial visitation. I have given numerous lectures at UFO conventions at Woodbridge, and attended many more as a guest of author and formidable researcher John Hanson: I've also had the pleasure of acting as MC and moderator for Col. Halt at one of these. I have come away from these experiences with an opinion of the whole 'UFO scene' that may surprise – even upset – a few people.

I've reached the conclusion that the attendees and participants at these events can be categorised as follows:

Group One

People who have a genuine interest in the subject, either as a result of a personal experience, or through wide background research. They are often looking for explanations, support or even closure. This group includes people who seem to be genuine abductees, people who have experienced close encounters with strange aerial objects and contactees who feel they may actually have seen or met their occupants.

Group Two

People who are making a living (sometimes modest, sometimes substantial) from writing books and making appearances to talk about the UFO phenomenon and the paranormal in general: some, at least, do not seem to have any genuine personal experience or enthusiasm for the subject other than the pursuit of a second income!

Group Three

What is possibly the largest group is made up of what might most politely be described as cultists: people (often with little or no scientific background) who claim all manner of arcane inside knowledge, including how flying discs function, who operates them and where they originate. They see evidence of cover-ups and conspiracies everywhere, even in the most mundane of events. They give their support to famous (or notorious!) personalities within the field, but can switch allegiancies at the drop of a hat! Members of this group can become aggressive and often respond negatively to any form of contradiction or criticism. Of course, TV documentary makers focus on this subset because its members make terrific television: these are the individuals who are seen with their heads wrapped in aluminium foil, pointing electric heaters at the night skies and 'trance communicating' with inhabitants of the most unlikely home planets...

Which group do I belong to? I'd like to feel it's group one: as an astronomer, one-time pilot and birdwatcher, I have seen and photographed over a dozen perplexing objects in the sky (and on the ground!) I have spoken to a large number of credible witnesses: pilots, astronauts, police officers and so on, but also plenty of ordinary folk who have had extraordinary experiences. Like them, I look forward to some form of explanation – disclosure, even – in my lifetime. It is, of course, the case that I have given many lectures and written a number of books on the subject of UFOs (as well as the paranormal and historical conspiracies) and have made numerous TV and radio appearances: but I charge only expenses for my talks and have sold barely enough books to cover my costs. Interestingly, most people to whom I reveal my interest in the topic immediately dump me in the third group! This seems to be the case with all serious researchers (whether concert violinists, ex-MOD civil servants or retired police officers). So much so, that one might almost believe it was a strategy first initiated as part of a cover up. There's a conspiracy theory for you!

OUR FORBIDDEN MOON

APPENDIX 6

HOW COULD ANYTHING THIS BIG BE KEPT SECRET?

IN 1978 a film was released that would eventually achieve cult status: 'Capricorn One'

The basic story line (spoiler alert!) is that, with just a short time to go before launch, serious system problems are identified on the USA's first manned mission to Mars: with no time - or real idea - how to correct these, senior figures at NASA decide to go ahead with the mission, removing the unsuspecting astronaut crew from their spacecraft moments before lift-off.

The three men are whisked away to a secret location where a set has been constructed to simulate the surface of Mars: here, the voyage to the red planet, the landing and exploration and the return to Earth months later are all staged in a studio. At some point it occurs to the astronauts that there is no way they will be allowed to complete a successful return to Earth....

I won't divulge the rest of the plot: if you haven't watched it yet, you really should!

Of relevance to us is the fact that every possible objection to the idea that the Apollo missions were faked and the fact kept secret are successfully addressed by the film.

For example, as it enters orbit all the various downlinks from the spacecraft have to arrive at the appropriate Controller in Mission Control. The major 'desks' were

CAPCOM – The Capsule Communicator was generally the only person who communicated directly with the astronauts

SURGEON – Flight Surgeon (maintained a check on crew health and physical performance)

BOOSTER – Booster Systems Engineer (monitored the launch rocket until capsule separation)

RETRO – Retrofire Officer (responsible for abort decisions, orbital insertion and retrofire burns)

GUIDANCE – Guidance Officer (responsible for onboard computers and navigation)

FIDO – Flight Dynamics Officer (monitored the ascent trajectory of the launch vehicle)

EECOM – Electrical, Environmental, and Consumables Management (monitored fuel cells, cabin cooling, electrical systems etc)

GNC – Guidance, Navigation and Control Systems Engineer (responsible for the control system used to steer the spacecraft and for the Service Module main engine)

TELMU – Officer who oversaw telemetry and electrical systems, and mobility during EVAs

CONTROL – Flight Controller

PROCEDURES – The Organization and Procedures ensured mission policy and rules were followed.

OUR FORBIDDEN MOON

INCO – Integrated Communications Officer

FAO – Flight Activities Officer

NETWORK – This desk supervised communications with global ground stations

RECOVERY – The Recovery Supervisor co-ordinated recovery of the Command Module after splashdown.

Each desk largely operated independently, the controllers monitoring their own data and looking for irregularities or deviations from the planned mission profile. If an emergency did arise, the Flight Director could instantly call for data from any desk.

OUR FORBIDDEN MOON

The assumption made in 'Capricorn One' is that a Controller would not question the data on his screen unless it suddenly deviated from what was expected: as long, say, as the FIDO received a steady stream of data that reflected what was anticipated at any stage of the Saturn V's climb to orbit, he wouldn't question where it was coming from. Despite what some writers claim, the distance from the Earth to the Moon is so small (in Astronomical terms!) that a radio signal from the lunar surface would have reached Mission Control in around 1.3 seconds: had it really originated in Earth orbit, the difference in reception times would have gone unnoticed. Except... I often wonder whether there was a delay circuit purposely included in NASA's communications systems. After all, broadcasts from space missions were often live: suppose something really ghastly had occurred? Would NASA have wanted images of an onboard fire and all that would have entailed being put out live on primetime TV? I doubt it!

It is at least possible that all but a few key controllers could have been happily checking data streams and comms that originated in Earth orbit or even (relayed via a satellite) from a studio somewhere.

Obviously at least some of the 'Close-out Crew' who had the job of sealing the Astronauts in their spacecraft would have needed to be in on the scam, but the launch tower was cleared a couple of hours before: plenty of time for a flight crew to slip out and be spirited away!

All the data during an actual lunar mission could have been transmitted from Earth orbit or a studio, right up until re-entry and splashdown. The crew could have either re-entered from orbit or – if the whole mission had been a simulation – they could have been loaded into the Command Module which was then dropped out of the back of a transport aircraft. (To land, possibly, within a few kilometres of the recovery vessel!)

If you work this through, it seems as if just a few hundred people would need to know that a deception had been carried out. Compare this with

OUR FORBIDDEN MOON

the decryption of the German 'Enigma' and Japanese 'Purple' signals traffic during World War 2, the development of the Colossus computer at Bletchley Park, the Manhattan Project and other top secrets. Most of these, despite the huge numbers of people working on them, were maintained as ultra secret until years after the event.

At Groom Lake (AKA Area 51) in Nevada, generation after generation of new, high-performance aircraft are developed, tested and flown with hardly a hint of their existence reaching the outside world. You can bank on it that replacements for the SR-71, B2 and F117 have been operational for years without their details being leaked.

Is this a lunar landscape? No. It's a crater field at Groom Lake, Nevada, created by nuclear weapon testing. But it could easily have been used for lunar mission simulations.

OUR FORBIDDEN MOON

The true number of casualties and fatalities during warfare and natural disasters are sometimes understated so as not to damage morale (The deaths following Hurricane Andrew in Florida being a recent example)

So: could a major event exposed to the full glare of the media be a complete fabrication? As we have seen, the 'Starwars' program is a good example. Can a huge undertaking be kept secret from the public indefinitely?

Would a government or 'black ops' program take such steps to defend their own hidden agendas? It would seem so!

Glossary

Astronaut

The term used by the United States for its space travellers and those that enter space in its spacecraft.

CAPCOM

At the time of the Apollo missions only one person generally spoke to the astronauts in space: this was the Capsule Communicator. From the early 1960s the Mission Control Centre was based at the Johnson Space Centre in Texas, and it became usual for CAPCOM to use the call sign 'Houston'

Cislunar cis-lunar space

This is the volume of space that would be enclosed by a sphere centred on the Earth with the Earth-Moon distance as its radius.

CM / Command Module

The crew compartment of any spacecraft constructed in several parts. In the case of the Gemini and Apollo spacecraft, the astronauts spent most of their time in the CM and returned to Earth inside it. Soviet / Russian spacecraft feature a similar re-entry capsule.

Cosmonaut

The term used by the Soviet Union and latterly Russia for their space travellers and those that enter space in its spacecraft.

EBE / Extraterrestrial biological entity

This term is preferred by many writers for visitors from other worlds or dimensions.

EVA / Extravehicular activity

As early as the Gemini and Voskhod Programs in the mid 1960s, space travellers (attached by tethers) would occasionally leave their spacecraft to conduct experiments. The term was carried forward during the Apollo missions, and included any procedure on the lunar surface.

Flight roster

From the start of the US space program crews were selected on aptitude and seniority. As Group 1 and 2 Astronauts began carrying out additional missions, the Head of the Astronaut Office produced a rolling list of who would be given future missions. Poor attitude or performance, injury and sickness or changing mission parameters could alter the roster (For example, on Apollo 13)

Gemini

The United State's two-man spacecraft, generally regarded as the most reliable the US ever produced. It consisted of a Command Module (with ejector seats rather than an escape rocket) and a Service Module. This had two components: one held life support, power and communications equipment, the other steering and retro-rockets.

Heatshield

When returning to Earth from orbit or cislunar space, a spacecraft has to reduce its velocity from thousands of kilometres per hour to perhaps 200, when parachutes can be deployed for landing. This is accomplished by reducing the spacecraft's velocity using retro-rockets, approaching the atmosphere at the correct angle, and allowing kinetic energy to be dissipated by friction with the atmosphere. This generates vast amounts of heat, producing temperatures of thousands of degrees centigrade. To withstand this, most spacecraft approach the atmosphere with surfaces constructed to lose heat by ablation. In the case of the Shuttle Orbiters, their outer surfaces were covered with three types of insulation in the form of thermal tiles or blankets.

Lunar Module / LM / LEM

The curiously-shaped Lunar Module was designed to carry two astronauts (the Commander and Lunar Module Pilot) to the surface of the Moon, provide living accommodation for the duration of the visit and return the astronauts to lunar orbit, where they would rendezvous with the Command Module.

Maria

The Moon is held in an orbit around the Earth that takes roughly 28 days to complete: this is also the time it takes for the Moon to rotate once on its axis. As a result, we see just over half of the Moon's surface, the far side facing permanently away from us. The side we can see is pock-marked with cometary and asteroidal impact craters as well as large, dark roughly circular features. In the early years of telescopic astronomy, these were assumed to be seas, and were named accordingly. (The word 'mare' is latin for 'sea') In fact, they are huge basalt-filled basins, created by massive impacts after the formation of the Earth-Moon system

Mercury Program

This was the United State's first manned spaceflight program. From 1961 until 1963, six American astronauts travelled into space in a tiny capsule not much larger than a phone box! The first two missions (those of Alan B Shepard and Ivan 'Gus' Grissom) were fifteen minute sub-orbital hops, using adapted Redstone IRBMs. The remaining missions (John Glenn, M Scott Carpenter, Walter Schirra and Leroy Gordon Cooper) were orbital flights.

Milky Way

On a clear night in a region with dark skies it is possible to see our Galaxy, a whirlpool-shaped mass of 300 billion stars. Our Sun is just one of these, situated out on the end of one of the spiral arms. There are thought to be 100 billion galaxies in the Universe!

NASA

This is the acronym for the US National Aeronautics and Space Administration. Created in 1958 following the disestablishment of the National Advisory Committee for Aeronautics, it is the organisation that has oversight of all civilian space programs in the USA

Regolith

This is the term used for a layer of crushed rock, dust and debris over a solid surface, typically found on the Moon, Mars, asteroids and the Earth

R&D

Research and development are the initial stages leading to a final production design.

Service Module / SM

This provided propulsion, electrical power and storage for water, oxygen and fuel during an Apollo mission. Before return from Earth orbit at the end of the mission, it was jettisoned, burning up in the atmosphere.

Taikonaut

The term used by China for its space travellers and those that enter space in its spacecraft.

OUR FORBIDDEN MOON

A mountain near Taurus Littrow, allegedly taken during the Apollo 17 mission, compared with a hill near the summit of Muana Kea, Hawaii, where astronaut geological training took place, and a still from '2001, a Space Odyssey'

OUR FORBIDDEN MOON

BIBLIOGRAPHY

'Somebody Else Is On The Moon', George Leonard, Pocket Books, 1977

'The Day After Roswell', Col. Philip J. Corso, Pocket Books, 1997

'Dark Mission', Richard C. Hoagland & Mike Bara, Feral House, 2007

'Alien Liaison', Timothy Goode, Random Century, 1991

'Dark Moon', Mary Bennett & David S. Percy, Aulis, 1999

'Haunted Skies, Volume 8', John Hanson & Dawn Holloway, Haunted Skies Publishing, 2013

The author with USAF veterans of the 1980 Rendlesham Forest Incident: John Burroughs and James Penniston, and author and former MoD UFO Desk Officer Nick Pope

Image Credits

Introduction photo   David Bryant

Plate 1, page 13   David Bryant

Plate 2, page 22   NASA

Plate 3. page 26   David Bryant

Plate 4, page 31   NASA

Plate 5, page 47   David Bryant

Plate 6, page 55   David Bryant

Plate 7, page 58   David Bryant

Plate 8, page 62   David Bryant

Plate 9, page 66   David Bryant

Plate 10, page 67   David Bryant

Plate 11, page 70   NASA

Plate 11, page 74   NASA

Plate 12, page 82   David Bryant, (from original by Stephen O'Meara)

Plate 13, page 84   David Bryant

Plate 14, page 91   David Bryant, John Hanson, Paola Harris

Plate 15, page 94   BBC

Plate 16, page 99	NASA
Plate 17, page 105	NASA
Plate 18, page 108	David Bryant
Plate 19, page 109	David Bryant
Plate 20, page 110	NASA/David Bryant
Plate 21, page 111	NASA
Plate 22, page 116	David Bryant (CGI)
Plate 23, page 118	David Bryant (CGI)
Plate 24, page 121	David Bryant
Plate 25, page 124	David Bryant
Plate 26, page 125	David Bryant
Plate 27, page 131	NASA
Plate 28, page 133	National Nuclear Security Administration (NNSA)
Plate 29, page 139	NASA / MGM Studios
Plate 30, page 142	Linda Bryant
Plate 31, page 145	David Bryant
Plate 32, page 146	David Bryant
Plate 33, page 147	David Bryant
Plate 34, page 148	David Bryant

The author with an authentic Apollo LiOH cartridge and a photograph showing how a square peg allegedly was made to fit a round hole during the Apollo 13 mission.

OUR FORBIDDEN MOON

General Thomas Stafford (Apollo 10 Cdr) selecting items from the author's display for the Stafford Air and Space Museum

Author, David Bryant and Astronaut Buzz Aldrin

OUR FORBIDDEN MOON

David Bryant with astronaut spacesuit at Stargazing Live

UNINVITED COMPANIONS

By David Bryant *(Foreword by Lionel Fanthorpe)*

168 pages, some in colour

Uninvited Companions is an examination of the paranormal phenomena known as orbs: the strange spheres of light that frequently appear on video and still photographs or are even, at times, seen by the unaided eye. With a BSc in Biological Sciences and Astronomy and a lifetime as a teacher and lecturer, author David Bryant has reached some new and startling conclusions about these contentious objects! The book examines other, apparently unrelated paranormal happenings, and consider whether they might be linked in some way to the orb phenomenon.

THE CONSPIRACY CONSPIRACY

By David Bryant (Foreword by Ray Kohn)

176 pages, many in colour

For far longer than you might imagine, politicians, dictators and other ruling elites have fully understood this basic principle: if you control what people hear, see and read, you control what they believe! If, through control of education, you can also erode people's analytical powers, and make them virtually uncritical, so much the better.

Many years ago I started to consider the idea that the deployment of the phrase and concept 'Conspiracy Theory' was part of a carefully considered strategy. It seemed to me that labelling any new thinking about a contentious issue as part of a 'Conspiracy Theory' was a great way of hiding some genuine but inconvenient truths among a rag-bag collection of urban legends, myths and fantasies.

In each chapter of this book, I examine some of the modern sacred cows of institutionalized belief and consider to what extent they are subverted to manipulate public opinion and attitudes – and why! I use examples from my own experiences where possible: at least I can be certain these are true!

In conclusion, this book is intended as an attempt to encourage its readers to think more deeply about how and why we respond to the frequent – and often conflicting – pronouncements of the many experts who affect and regulate all of our lives.

DANGER FROM THE SKIES
By David Bryant *(Foreword by Dr Rob Bryant)*
132 pages, some in colour

Does Mankind's nemesis lurk out in deep space, beyond the edge of the Solar System?

Danger From The Skies offers a completely new 'spin' on the effect of major impact events on the evolution of life on Earth and the objects that caused them. Darwinian theory alone cannot adequately explain the sudden disappearance of highly successful groups such as the trilobites, dinosaurs and giant Pleistocene mammals: what factor is missing from the textbooks? With a background in Biological Sciences and Astronomy and as the UK's only full-time meteorite dealer, author David Bryant has reached some startling and novel conclusions about the causes of mass extinctions. The book examines the evidence for past planet-shattering impacts and discusses what – if anything – can be done to prevent such an event in the future.

David Bryant at his display of meteorites available through Spacerocks UK

SPACEROCKS

By David Bryant *(Foreword by Nik Szymoneck)*

160 pages, many in colour

An up-to-date and very popular collectors' pocket guide to meteorites: their classification, composition and history, accessible also to students of all ages wishing to know more about this fascinating subject. It describes what meteorites tell us about the formation of the solar system and how they have contributed to our understanding of planetary structure. Fully illustrated with photos, charts and diagrams!

www.ingramcontent.com/pod-product-compliance
Lightning Source LLC
Chambersburg PA
CBHW061111070526
44583CB00027B/3259